ORGANISATION AND MANAGEMENT OF PUBLIC DISTRIBUTION SYSTEM

ORGANISATION AND MANAGEMENT OF Public Distribution System

By

ANURADHA SHARMA

ANMOL PUBLICATIONS PVT. LTD.
NEW DELHI - 110 002 (INDIA)

ANMOL PUBLICATIONS PVT. LTD.
4374/4B, Ansari Road, Daryaganj
New Delhi - 110 002
www.anmolbooks.com

Organisation and Management of Public Distribution System

First Edition, 2002

ISBN 81-261-1038-4

PRINTED IN INDIA

Published by J.L. Kumar for Anmol Publications Pvt. Ltd., New Delhi - 110 002 and Printed at Mehra Offset Press, Delhi.

Contents

	Foreword	*vii*
	Acknowledgements	*viii*
	Preface	*xi*
	List of Tables	*xii*
Chapter–1	Introductory and Research Methodology	1
Chapter–2	Review of Literature	41
Chapter–3	The Administration and the Organisation of PDS	60
Chapter–4	Operational Aspects of the Fair Price Shops	105
Chapter–5	The Consumer and the PDS	127
Chapter–6	Problems, Conclusion and Suggestions	182
	Bibliography	217

Foreword

I thank you for having sent to me manuscript of your book titled "Organisation and Management of Public Distribution System".

I have gone through your thesis which has covered essential aspects of the relevant subject.

Studies of the type carried out by you serve a useful purpose as national security in present times encompasses economic security including food security, besides security from the usual types of external and internal threats. I would agree that public distribution system has to reach out to the right targets, minimise the chances of pilferage or other types of corruption, take adequate care of the storage problems and reduce the element of subsidy to the barest minimum required.

Raj Bhavan
April 27, 2001

—Girish Chandra Saxena
Governor
Jammu & Kashmir

Acknowledgements

No praise can be too high for, and no words can be adequate to the intellectual support and guidance I have received from my mentor Dr. Keshav Sharma, Reader, Department of Commerce, University of Jammu, Jammu. His constant academic and moral support and able guidance had made it possible for me to complete this research work.

I am deeply beholden to Hon'ble Shri Girish Chandra Saxena, Governor of Jammu & Kashmir for writing a Foreword to this book.

I must express my gratitude to all my teachers of the Department of Commerce especially Prof. P.N. Abrol and Prof. R.D Sharma, Head of the Department for providing me with all help in the completion of this work.

Sincere gratitude is also expressed to Prof. A.N. Sadhu, Department of Economics, University of Jammu and Dr. Deepak Gupta, Department of Management Studies for their valuable suggestions and guidance at various stages during my work on the subject. I am also thankful to the librarians of the Department of Economics and Management Studies for providing me all the necessary help.

A staunch and open minded liberal, Prof. Anil C. Itteyrah has encouraged me to put across my point of view freely and without inhibition. I am thankful to him for all the support and valuable time given by him in my endeavour.

I would also like to acknowledge the help rendered by Prof. M. Sayeed, who had a profound influence on my way of thinking.

I acknowledge with thanks the contribution and the co-operation of the officials of the Food and Supplies Department, Jammu Division and the Food Corporation of India, Jammu; librarian I.C.S.S.R, New Delhi; librarian RTL, Delhi School of Economics; and librarian Indian Institute of Public Administration, New Delhi.

I am also grateful to all the respondents and other people who came forward to talk about their perceptions of PDS to complete the survey work most sincerely and under very tiring circumstances.

The scholarship provided by the University of Jammu, Jammu is duly acknowledged.

I am also beholden to all my friends especially Ms. Poonam Rasotra, Dr. Gurmeet Singh, Mr. Vinod Kaul, Mrs. Seema Murtaza, Mr. Mubassir Latifi, Mr. Amarjit Singh, Mrs. Anita Kaul who provided me with all encouragement during the periods of stress and strain in the process of completing my research work.

I doubt that this work would have ever been completed had it not been for the insistence, whole-hearted co-operation and encouragement of my husband Mr. Anil Khajuria. I have also enjoyed the everlasting encouragement, love, affection and blessings of my mother-in-law Mrs. Raj Khajuria. She throughout kept me patting while I was doing the present work and never let me lose the courage. I don't have to thank her. Instead I have to bow my head down before her in esteem and respect.

I am thankful to Mrs. Vijay Laxmi Sharma who has been sisterly in having given me all love and affection during the course of the study.

Last but not the least, I wish to express my heartfelt

appreciation to many who have contributed to this project both explicitly and implicitly.

The Almighty always blessed me with all the inner strength which I so badly required at moments when I felt slightly derailed from the track. It is He who has disposed the proposed.

(ANURADHA SHARMA)

Preface

Public Distribution System (PDS) and its predecessor, the Rationing System, have remained with us since World War II. From emergency and temporary war measure to a deliberate social policy instrument, it has seen many ups and downs during the later half of this century. During this period, the Rationing System has evolved from a distribution programme for scarce commodities into the present day Public Distribution System (PDS) with its emphasis on subsidised prices. The Five Year Plan documents have repeatedly stressed that the PDS is a deliberate social policy instrument and forms part of the permanent strategy of the Government to ensure adequate availability of foodgrains at reasonable prices to safeguard the interests of the vulnerable sections of the society. The PDS, too, offers a discrete study to study the managerial and organisational imperatives and the social system dictating change. The cost of distribution need not to be minimum due to the several problems, divided control and absence of planning and co-ordination in the existing Public Distribution Organisation.

The present study is an attempt to analyse the policy framework and the organisational structure of the PDS at both the macro and the micro levels in the Jammu Region of the State of Jammu & Kashmir thus paving the way for the overall development of this system.

List of Tables

1.1	The procurement, Distribution and Stock Position of Wheat and Rice	8
1.2	Sanctioned Rationed Scales in Jammu Division	9
1.3	Distributise Population covered by the Department and the Projected Population of 1990	11
1.4	Rationed Population	12
1.5	Off-take of Foodgrains from Govt. Depots	12
1.6	Import of Foodgrains	13
1.7	Allotment & Lifting of Wheat and Rice in Jammu Division	13
1.8	Allocation of Commodities by F.C.I.	17
1.9	District-wise Despatches of Foodgrains	19
1.10	District-wise off-take of Foodgrains	20
1.11	District-wise number of Fair Price Shops	21
1.12	District-wise Despatches of Foodgrains to the Depots in Jammu Region	24
1.13	Utilization of Foodgrains under the RPDS	29
1.14	Quantities of Ration Foodgrains dumped in Departmental Godowns	30
1.15	Educational Background, Income & Occupation of the Respondents who purchase the Ration items	36
3.1	The Administrative Functional Framework	65

3.2	Important Decisions at Various Levels	66
3.3	Rationed Price of Food-items	74
3.4	Responses of the Agencies regarding the Main Causes for Origin of PDS policy and Govt. Objectives in Establishing Fair Price Shops	88
3.5	Responses of the Agencies regarding Services Rendered by the Fair Price Shops	92
3.6	Responses of the Agencies regarding Awareness about Production-cum-Distribution System Under the PDS.	94
3.7	Responses of the Agencies regarding following the same Norms and Conditions in Urban & Rural Areas	96
3.8	Responses of the Agencies regarding Awareness about the policies of Revamped PDS	98
3.9	Responses of the Agencies regarding Awareness about the Objectives & Working of FCI	100
4.1	Responses regarding Total Cards Served	108
4.2	Responses regarding Main Objectives of the FPS Dealers	112
4.3	Responses regarding Satisfaction with Monthly Salary/Commission of Dealers	114
4.4	Responses regarding Rating the Behaviour of Customers	115
4.5	Responses regarding Experiences while dealing with Customers	116
4.6	Responses regarding Providing adequate Services to Customers	118
4.7	Responses regarding Prevention in providing Better Services to Customers	120
4.8	Responses regarding Consumers Consuming the Ration Items	122

4.9	Responses regarding Reasons for purchasing Ration Items from the Dealers' Point of View	123
4.10	Response regarding Selling Packed products	124
4.11	Responses regarding Dealing in a Larger Range of Products	124
5.1	Educational level of the Respondents	128
5.2	Occupation of the Respondents	128
5.3	Respondents of Different Age groups	137
5.4	Respondents of Different Income group	137
5.5	Responses Generated regarding Objectives. of Govt.in establishing FPSs under the PDS	140
5.6	Responses regarding Frequency of Purchasing Food Items from the FPs	142
5.7	Responses regarding Purchasing Items mainly from the FPS	143
5.8	Responses Generated regarding Distance between Residence & the FPS	144
5.9	Responses Generated regarding Satisfaction with the Location of FPS	145
5.10	Responses Generated regarding Availability of Ration Commodities in Time	146
5.11	Responses regarding Satisfaction with Weighing Process in FPS	148
5.12	Responses regarding Time Consumption to draw Ration from the FPS	149
5.13	Responses regarding Reasons for preference to purchase Food Items From the FPS than the Open Market	150
5.14	Responses regarding Consumer Preference for Different Food Items	154
5.15	Responses regarding Quantity of the Ration Items Issued under the PDS	156

5.16	Responses regarding Basis For Issuing Ration Quota	157
5.17	Responses regarding Quality of Food Items Issued under the PDS	158
5.18	Responses regarding Satisfaction with Pricing System	159
5.19	Responses regarding Rating the Behaviour of FPS Dealers	160
5.20	Responses regarding Aware about Holidays at FPS	160
5.21	Responses regarding Problems by Co-incidence of Holidays	161
5.22	Responses regarding Reasons for Standing in Queue for such a Long Time	162
5.23	Responses regarding Experiences while Purchasing Food Items from FPS	166
5.24	Responses regarding Awareness about the Objectives of Consumer Councils	170
5.25	Responses regarding Improvement in Functioning of PDS through the Consumer Council	171
5.26	Responses regarding Contribution to Consumer Welfare Activities	172
5.27	Responses regarding Complaints about Functioning of FPSs	173
5.28	Responses regarding Lodging Complaints to Different Authorities	174
5.29	Responses regarding any Suggestions to Improve the Procedure of Issuing Ration Card	175
5.30	Responses regarding Suggestions to Avoid Delay & Quick disposal of Customers at the FPS	176
5.31	Responses regarding Suggestions to improve the overall Functioning of the PDS	180

6.1	Responses of Agencies regarding main Bottlenecks in the Conduct of Procurement Operations	184
6.2	Responses of the Agencies regarding Reasons for Storage Losses.	185
6.3	Responses of the Agencies regarding Defects in the Present PDS.	186
6.4	Responses regarding Receiving Customer Complaints	190
6.5	Responses regarding Satisfaction with the Present System of distribution from Dealers' Point of View.	192
6.6	Responses of the Agencies regarding Meeting Consumer Preference in terms of Taste, Variety, CO. etc.	204
6.7	Responses of the Agencies regarding the Organisational & Managerial Structure at the District Level.	206
6.8	Responses of the Agencies regarding Suggestions to Improve the Present Working of PDS.	208
6.9	Responses regarding Suggestions for Effective Management of PDS.	210

Chapter–1

Introductory and Research Methodology

1. INTRODUCTION

The distribution system encompasses all movements starting from the shipment of raw material to the delivery of the finished product to the consumer. The distribution system undertaken by the government or any public agency is termed as "Public Distribution System" (PDS). A PDS is the whole or a part of the distribution system in principle owned and controlled by the public authorities on behalf of the general public and run by them for the good of the general public or a specific group thereof.

"Public Distribution" is an aspect of the demand and supply management[1]. The PDS is based on the following broad guidelines:

(i) A continuous and permanent system of public distribution;

(ii) A comprehensive coverage of the vulnerable sections;

(iii) Coverage of both deficit as well as surplus states;

(iv) Distribution of such quantities as will not erode the consumption standards of the poorest;

(v) Charging a price that the vulnerable sections can afford; and

(vi) Check holding and blackmarketing of essential commodities[2].

2. ORIGIN AND HISTORY OF PDS

Evolution of public distribution of foodgrains in India has its origin in the 'rationing' system introduced by the British during World War II.[3]

The PDS in India forms an important part of state strategy for intervening in the distribution of foodgrains and other essential commodities. However the nature of the policy of state's intervention is largely determined by the causes and conditions which are responsible for its emergence and growth. Therefore, the major causes of the origin of this policy are:

(i) Drought, famine and war conditions;

(ii) Inflation;

(iii) Market imperfections;

(iv) Poverty; and

(v) Lack of distributive justice.

The state intervention in the distributive mechanism for the first time took place in the year 1939 at the beginning of the Second World War in the form of the imposition of controls. Among the foodgrains, wheat was the first important item to be brought under control. The food control order was promulgated in May 1942. In the same year, due to the occurrence of Bengal famine, the fair price shop scheme was converted into the "Rationing System". In 1943, the first Foodgrains Policy Committee stressed the need for continuing the rationing and recommended maintenance of a reserve stock and inclusion of the rural areas under the rationing scheme. Two further developments in the history of the evolution of the control system are:

— The increasing emphasis being laid on organising strong and wide network of PDS, and

— The increasing administrative control over the price and distribution of many key products in lieu of the statutory or formal control[4].

Public distribution of foodgrains was retained as deliberate social policy by India, when it embarked on the path of a planned economic development in 1951. It was, infact an important component of the policy of growth with justice.[5] The real aim was price stability for the urban consumers.

Public Distribution of grains was retained as a deliberate social policy by India, when it embarked on the path of a planned economic development in 1951. It was, infact an important component of the policy of growth with justice, The real aim was price stability for the urban consumers.

This trend continued in the Second Plan which spoke of building food reserves to moderate price fluctuations and to meet emergencies.

And though the strategy was reiterated in the Third Plan, there was still no effort to evolve a conscious policy of providing 'food for all' to which the First Plan had made a reference.

The Fourth Plan continued the trend and further, got caught up in the ideology of co-operatives replacing fair price shops instead of emphasising the need for making food grains available to all the poor at affordable prices.

The Fifth Plan looked at the PDS as an instrument to discourage speculative activities in the area of trading and stipulated that it should avoid any sizable subsidy burden on the public exchequer.

The Sixth Five Year Plan (1980-85) made a general reference to the need for the PDS to play a major role in ensuring supplies of essential commodities to consumers at reasonable prices. It promised that the PDS would be so developed that it would remain a stable and permanent feature of the strategy to control prices and to achieve equitable distribution.

While the Seventh Plan pinned its faith on decentralised agricultural production, especially in regions hitherto undeveloped, to provide higher rural incomes and meet inflationary pressures, its concept of an expanded food security system also included public procurement, buffer stocking and public distribution. Finally, the plan linked the main thrust of the system to poverty in as much as it spokes of its expansion in the rural areas with special attention to remote and inaccessible areas, so that the PDS becomes supplementary to the poverty alleviation programme[6].

Creation of Food Corporation of India and Agricultural Prices Commission in 1965 consolidated the position of PDS. Government was now committed to announce a minimum support price for wheat and paddy and procure quantities that could not fetch even such minimum prices in the market. The resultant stocks were to be utilised for maintaining distribution through the PDS and a position of these were used to create and maintain buffer stocks. All through the ups and downs of Indian agriculture, PDS was continued as a deliberate social policy of the Government with the objectives of:

(i) Providing food grains and other essential items to vulnerable sections of the society at reasonable (subsidized) price;

(ii) To have a moderating influence on the open market prices of cereals; and

(iii) To attempt socialisation in the matter of distribution of essential commodities.

The PDS seeks to provide to the beneficiaries two cereals i.e. rice and wheat and four essential commodities, viz., sugar, edible oil, soft coke and kerosene oil. However, state governments which actually manage the system at the ground level, are exhorted to add other essential commodities like pulses, salt, candles, matchboxes, ordinary cloth, school copies and the like.[7]

3. NEED FOR PDS

For a common man, even in a land of honey and milk, there is no assurance of deliverance from hunger unless these charged with the task of governing him take conscious and deliberate steps to channel that abundance in his direction so that he can absorb the little that he needs.[8] One of the major objectives of planning in India has been to provide 'National' minimum level of living to its subjects. This requires provision of not only the needed quantum of food grains but also the required quality of food. The Government of India has adopted the dual market mechanism to meet the situation.[9] The Five Year Plan documents have repeatedly stressed that the PDS is a deliberate social policy instrument and forms part of the permanent strategy of the Government to ensure adequate availability of food grains for such poor households who come forward and take advantage of the system. The liberalisation of the Indian economy, set in motion in the past few years, has generated renewed interest in social safety-net programmes such as PDS.[10]

4. THE PDS POLICY/STRATEGY

The Distribution Policy of the Government usually evolves in response to the exigencies of critical situations such as shortages, price rise or quality deterioration of essential commodities. Because of its exigent nature, the Distribution Policy of the Government tends to be some what fragmented. Although concerns are often expressed for a consistent, well-integrated public distribution policy, the situational factors have prevented the emergence of such a comprehensive policy so far.[11] A systematic model of distribution Policy is shown in Fig 1.

By and large, this policy has not changed. The procurement, buffer stocking and the PDS of Foodgrains have been important instruments of implementing the Food Policy. While PDS takes care of the objective of distributing foodgrains, among others, to the poor, procurement acts as a system of support to farmers. Stocks can be used to reduce inflationary pressures. Even though these objectives have been achieved with varying degrees of successes, at present only the interests of the farmers seem to be taken care of by this procurement-PDS-bufferstocking operations.[12]

An effective PDS requires the fulfilment of certain conditions regarding the size of total supplies, the range of commodities to be included under it and an appropriate, non-arbitrary distribution of these rationed commodities among various regions and sections of society. Making available the six essential commodities (rice, wheat, sugar, edible oil, soft coke and kerosene oil) to the state Governments is the responsibility of the Central Government Taking commodities other than cereals (rice and wheat) first, the arrangement for such supply is as under:

Sugar: Central Government under the provisions of the Essential Commodities Act, fixes a levy percentage and accordingly every sugar factory has to deliver the percentage of production to the Government. Presently, the levy is 40%. Central Government allots to the State Government every month their share of the sugar out of the overall levy quantity on the basis of 425 gms/Capita on 1991 population basis.

Edible Oil: Whenever production of oilseeds dips and prices of edible oils rise steeply making it too expensive for poor people, Central Government imports oils like Palmoelin or rapeseed through its trading agencies and allots it among State Governments who sell it through PDS.

Soft Coke: Soft coke is allotted to the State Government from out of the stocks held by the public sector coal companies.

Kerosene Oil: The supply to the State Governments, on the basis of allocations made by the

Figure : 1

A Systematic Model of Distribution Policy

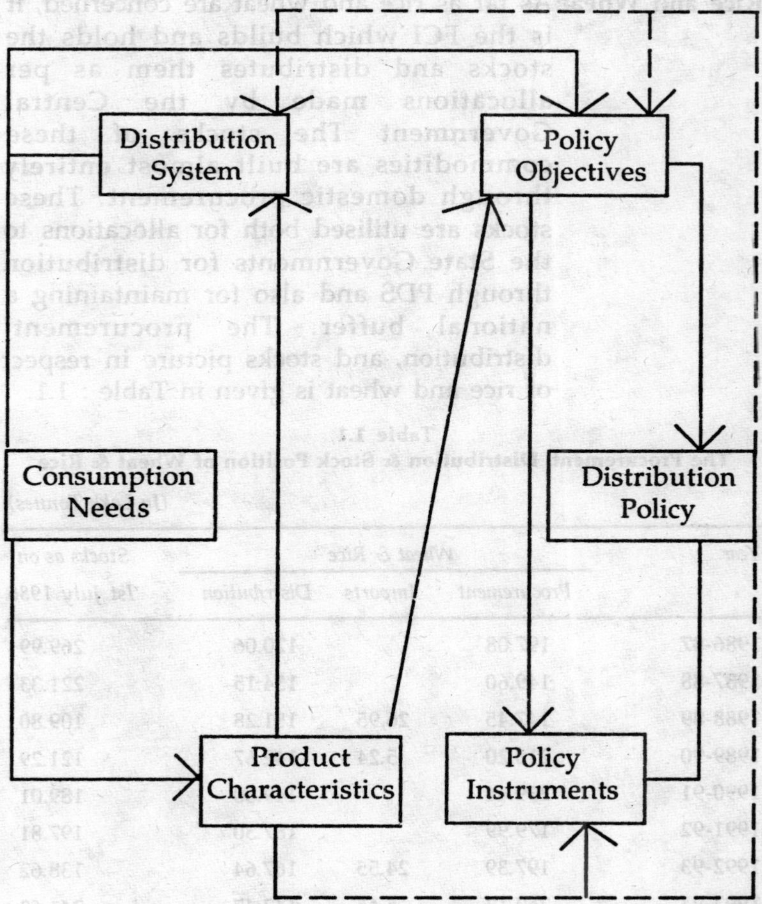

Central Government, is arranged by the Public Sector Oil Companies either from domestic production or by imports. It is also sold at subsidized rates.

Rice and Wheat: As far as rice and wheat are concerned, it is the FCI which builds and holds the stocks and distributes them as per allocations made by the Central Government The stocks of these commodities are built almost entirely through domestic procurement. These stocks are utilised both for allocations to the State Governments for distribution through PDS and also for maintaining a national buffer. The procurement, distribution, and stocks picture in respect of rice and wheat is given in Table : 1.1.

Table 1.1

The Procurement, Distribution & Stock Position of Wheat & Rice

(In Lakh Tonnes)

Year	*Wheat & Rice*			*Stocks as on*
	Procurement	*Imports*	*Distribution*	*Ist July 1986*
1986-87	197.08		120.06	269.99
1987-88	149.60		154.15	221.33
1988-89	147.45	26.95	151.28	109.80
1989-90	210.20	5.24	142.67	121.29
1990-91	239.44		149.60	189.01
1991-92	179.99		187.30	197.81
1992-93	197.39	24.55	167.64	138.62
1993-94	252.13	5.45	147.47	241.63

Source : Bulletins of the Ministry of Food, GOI, May-1994

Note:
1. 10 lakh = 1 million.
2. Imports shown in 1989-90 & 1993-94 are balance quantities received from out of contracts entered into during previous years.

It can safely be surmised that two or more successive years of good production will ease the open market prices, leaving up incentive for farmers and traders to hold back stocks and thereby result in good procurement. This situation will also reduce offtake and buffer stocks will be built up. On the other hand, two or more successive years of poor production will harden open market prices, give rise to speculative tendencies, reduce procurement, increase the demand on PDS resulting in heavy off take and lowering of stocks[13].

5. PDS IN JAMMU REGION

Food and supplies Department is mainly entrusted with the task of monitoring Public Distribution System under which food grains/levy sugar is issued to the rationees at the approved scale and uniform rates. Entire 1981 census population is being covered for providing the foodgrains. Accordingly, the present rationed population of Jammu Province is 29.48 lakh and sugar is being distributed at a uniform rate of 425 gms per head amongst 32.48 lakh population in the Division Distribution of rationed commodities i.e. wheat, atta, rice and sugar is being done through fair price outlets at the controlled rates every month. The scales of ration for each item are however, fixed per member of the family. This is illustrated in the following Table 1.2.

Table 1.2
Sanctioned Rationed Scales in Jammu Division
Rationed Scales Per Month Per Family Member

S.No.	*Category*	*Atta (Kgs)*	*Wheat (Kgs)*	*Rice (Kgs)*	*Sugar (Grams)*
1.	Jammu City	7.55	0.00	3.45	425
2.	Towns of Jammu Division	6.00	0.00	2.00	425
3.	Muffasils (FP) Shops	0.00	5.00	5.00	425*
4.	Kandi (For 3 Months)	0.00	10.00	0.00	0
5.	Gujjar & Bakkerwals	0.00	10.00	5.00	425*

* (Per Ration Card)

Source : As per the information recieved by the Food & Supplies Department, Jammu Division

Figure 2

Procurement distribution and Stocks (Wheat and Rice)

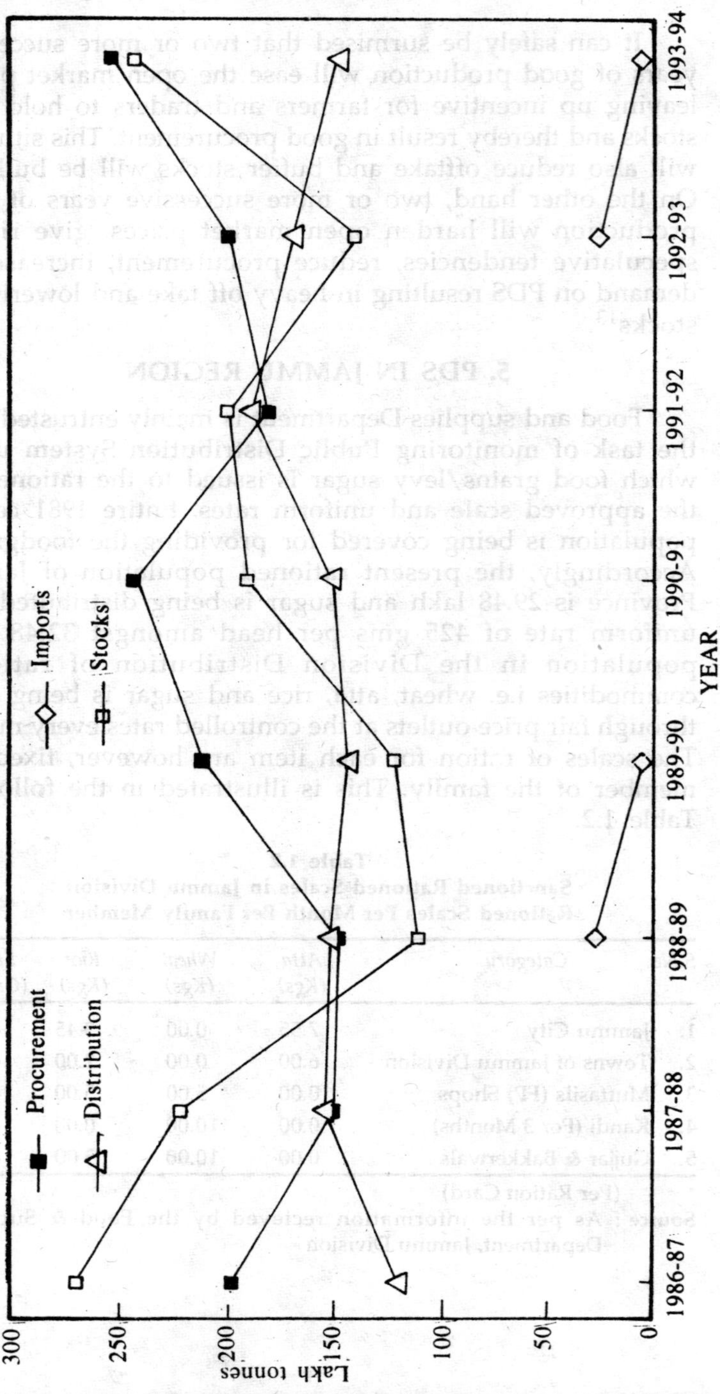

A statement indicating the distributise population covered by the department and the projected population of 1990 is as under in the form of Table 1.3.

Table 1.3
Distributise Population Covered by the Department and the Projected Population of 1990

(Fig in lacs)

S. No.	*Districts*	*Population Covered on the basis of 1981 Census Rationed Sugar*		*Projected Population ending 1990 Rationed Sugar*	
1	Jammu City	3.03	3.13	3.05	3.13
2	Jammu	7.52	9.01	9.15	9.15
3	Kathua	3.68	4.04	4.78	4.78
4	Udhampur	4.59	4.68	5.86	5.86
5	Rajouri	3.06	3.48	4.09	4.09
6	Poonch	2.25	2.39	2.87	2.87
7	Doda	4.16	4.51	5.18	5.18
Total		28.29	31.24	34.98	35.06
1	Gujjar & Bakerwals	0.94	0.94	0.94	0.94
2	Darbar Move Employees	0.09	0.09	0.09	0.09
3	Institutions	0.16	0.16	0.16	0.16
Total		1.19	1.19	1.19	1.19
Grand Total		29.48	32.43	36.17	36.25

Source : As per the Records of Food & Supplies Department, Jammu

Though food production in the State has gone up quite high from 58.31 lakh Qtls. in 1965-66 to 140.49 lakh Qtls. in 1991-92, it is yet to achieve self sufficiency and imports from outside the state continues. The following figures give data on year-wise imports of foodgrains from outside the state with the amount of subsidy given on the rationed supplies.

Year-wise rationed population in various towns, cities and Muffasils and off-take of foodgrains from Government depots are also given in Tables 1.4 & 1.5.

Table 1.4
Rationed Population

(Fig in lacs)

S. No.	Year	Cities	Towns	Muffasils Kandi Areas	Total
1.	1980-81	7.1	3.98	30.9	41.33
2.	1984-85	7.48	4.55	35.38	47.41
3.	1985-86	7.48	4.55	35.38	47.41
4.	1986-87	7.48	4.55	35.38	47.41
5.	1987-88	8.44	4.56	48.57	61.57
6.	1988-89	8.44	4.56	48.57	61.57
7.	1989-90	8.44	4.56	48.57	61.57
8.	1990-91	8.44	4.56	48.57	61.57*
9.	1991-92(p)	8.44	4.56	48.57	61.57*

Source : As per the Records of Digest of Statistics, J&k Govt, 1994

* : Includes Rationed Population of Pahari Areas, Bakerwals and Para Military Forces etc.

(P) : Provisional

Table 1.5
Off-take of Food Grains from Government Depots

(Fig in Lac Tonnes)

S.No.	Year	Rice	Wheat/Atta	Maize	Total
1.	1984-85	1.53	0.76	0.00	2.29
2.	1985-86	1.40	0.79	0.00	2.19
3.	1986-87	1.46	0.63	0.00	2.09
4.	1987-88	2.00	1.05	0.00	3.05
5.	1988-89	2.20	1.91	0.00	4.11
6.	1989-90	2.53	1.31	0.00	3.84
7.	1990-91	2.06	1.05	0.00	3.11
8.	1991-92	2.16	1.33	0.00	3.49

Source : Directorate of Food & Supplies, J&K Government

Table 1.6
Import of Food grains.

(Fig in Lac Tonnes)

S.No.	*Year*	*Rice*	*Wheat*
1.	1984-85	1.34	0.80
2.	1985-86	0.90	0.58
3.	1986-87	1.37	0.61
4.	1987-88	2.35	1.19
5.	1988-89	2.48	1.92
6.	1989-90	2.55	2.30
7.	1990-91	4.20	2.40
8.	1991-92	2.48	1.27

Source : Directorate of Food & Supplies, J&K

The annual requirement of wheat/Atta comes to 1.80 lakh tonnes whereas the annual requirements of rice comes to 0.60 lakh tonnes on the basis of 1981 census at the existing sanctioned ration scale. However, the off-take depends upon the crop production of the Division. Table 1.7 gives an idea of the allotment and lifting of the wheat and rice.

Table 1.7
Allotment & Lifting of Wheat & Rice in Jammu Division

	Wheat (Lac Tonnes)			*Rice (Lac Tonnes)*		
Year	*Allotment*	*Lifting*	*% age*	*Allotment*	*Lifting*	*% age*
1986-87	1.20	0.41	34	0.39	0.14	36
1987-88	1.41	0.75	53	0.52	0.17	33
1988-89	1.28	0.91	71	0.47	0.27	57
1989-90	1.84	0.72	40	0.38	0.23	59
1990-91	1.73	0.68	40	0.55	0.43	78
1991-92	1.82	0.72	40	0.40	0.22	58

Source : As per the Information received by the Directorate of Food & Supplies Department, Jammu.

Figure 3(a)

Population Covered by the Deptt. and Projected Population of 1990

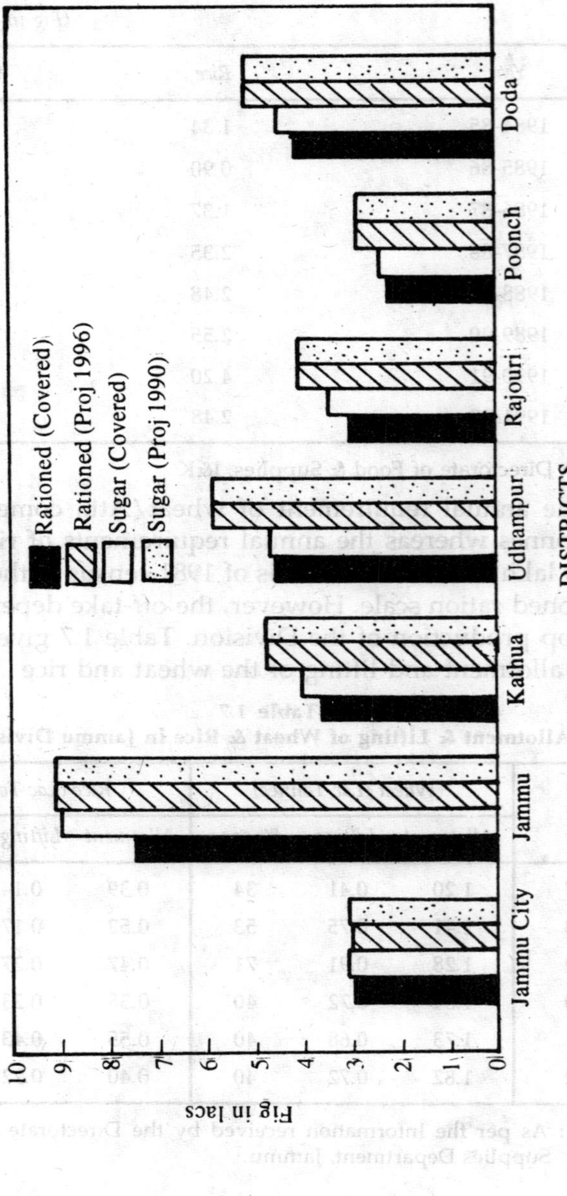

Figure 3(b)
Population Covered by the Deptt. and Projected Population of 1990

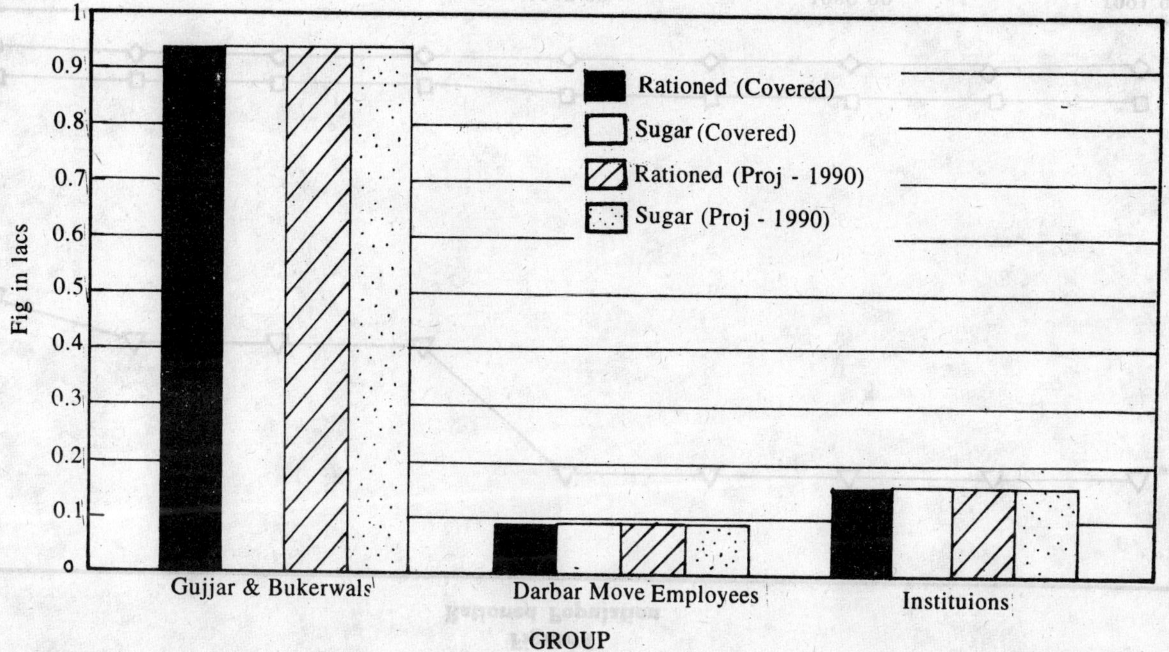

Figure 4
Rationed Population

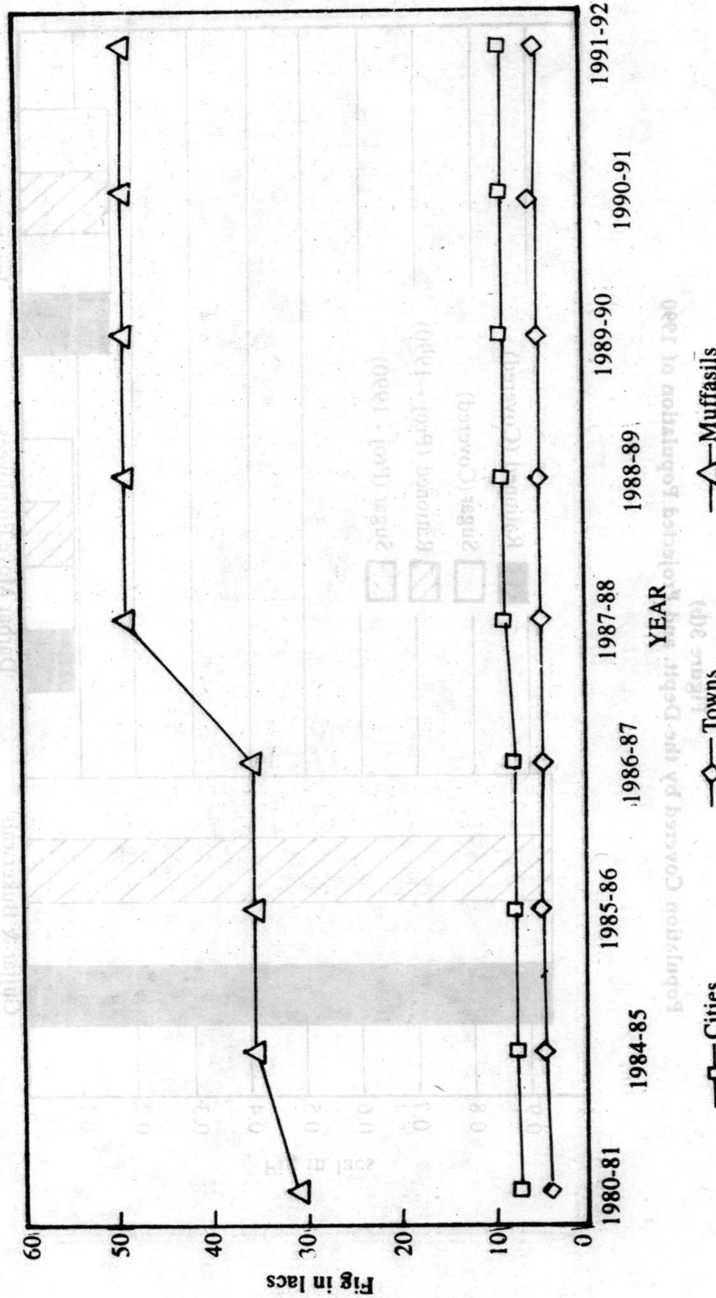

The Food Supplies Department gets supply of foodgrains/levy sugar from Food Corporation of India (FCI) for which allocation of each commodity is made by the Administrative Deptt. FCI has set up its depots at Jammu, Khillani in Doda, Govindsar in Kathua and at Rajouri. The depot at Rajouri has been commissioned in the month of October, 1992. The details of the commodities supplied by the FCI against the allocation during 1990-91 to 1992-93 are as under in the form of Table 1.8.

Table 1.8
Allocation of Commodities by FCI

(Figures in M.Tons)

S. No.	Commodity	Allocation			Receipt from FCI		
		1990-91	1991-92	1992-93	1990-91	1991-92	1992-93
1.	Wheat	144000	144000	144000	68290	88472	290397
2.	Rice	55000	76500	79821	42887	38460	37369
3.	Levy Sugar	16800	16800	16800	18141	16581	17172

Source : As per the Records of FCI, Regional Office, Jammu

Out of the supply position, the details of district-wise despatches of foodgrains/levy sugar during the year 1990-91 to 1992-93 are shown in Table 1.9. It reveals that the supply of foodgrains by FCI to the Directorate of Food & Supplies Deptt., Jammu has remained around 60% of the allocation which has kept the deptt. always in tight position, Moreover, the supply from FCI has remained always erratic and unplanned with the result that the Deptt. has been facing difficulties in monitoring the supply line in urban as well as rural areas in a uniform manner. District-wise off-take of foodgrains is also shown in Table 1.10.

Fair Price Shops in Jammu Division

Distribution of rationed commodities i.e. wheat, atta, rice and sugar is being done through a three-tier network of fair price outlets numbering 1552 outlets as on 31st March, 1993 as shown in Table 1.11.

Figure 5
Off-take of Foodgrains from Govt. Depots

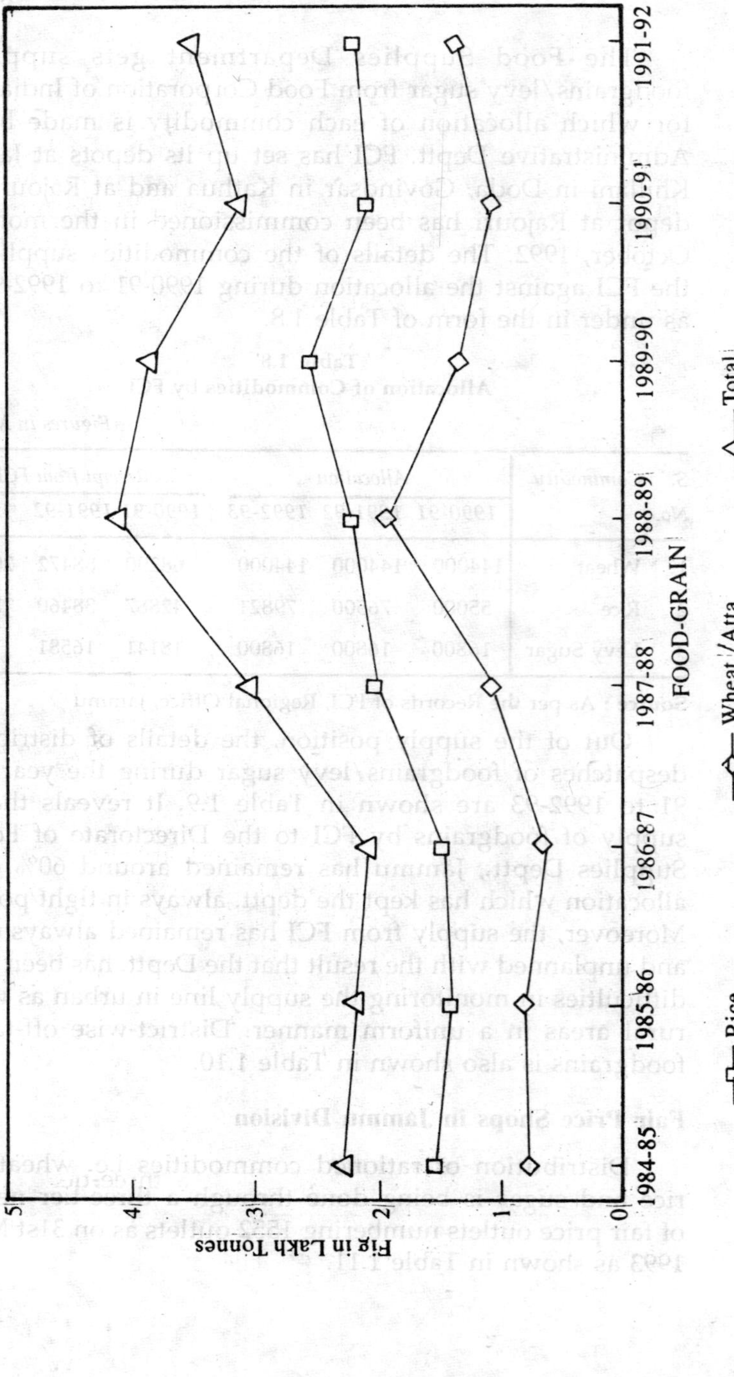

Table 1.9
District-Wise Despatches of Food Grains During 1990-91 to 1992-93

S. No.	Year	Jammu	Growth rate %	Kathua	Growth rate %	Udham-pur	Growth rate %	Rajouri	Growth rate %	Poonch	Growth rate %	Doda	Growth rate %
(a) ATTA													
1.	1990-91	21538		2008		4970		1659		1424		5203	
2.	1991-92	25486	18.33	2463	22.66	4687	–5.69	1881	13.38	1580	3.93	4670	–10.24
3.	1992-93	27903	13.82	2834	18.8	4819	–1.53	2066	11.59	1547	4.23	4617	–5.8
(b) WHEAT													
1.	1990-91	4946		2699		4055		1560		2097		15495	—
2.	1991-92	4352	–12.01	2327	–13.78	8556	111	1324	–15.13	2547	21.46	23258	50.1
3.	1992-93	1622	–42.73	2584	–2.15	8319	43.33	2223	19.37	2833	16.23	22431	20.32
(c) RICE													
1.	1990-91	24072		1213		5410		1466		2522		9305	—
2.	1991-92	20138	–16.34	1422	17.23	5964	10.24	1485	1.3	2316	–8.17	7720	–17.03
3.	1992-93	14288	–22.96	1516	11.79	9919	35.41	3076	44.85	1744	16.84	6500	–16.42
(d) SUGAR													
1.	1990-91	7317		2169		2466		1892		1306		2447	—
2.	1991-92	6897	–5.74	2137	–1.48	2552	3.49	1932	2.11	1345	2.97	2445	–0.08
3.	1992-93	7103	–1.47	2097	–1.67	3081	11.78	1900	0.21	1145	6.37	2356	–1.88

Source: As per the Survey Conducted.

Table 1.10

District-Wise Offtake of Food Grains During 1990-91 to 1992-93

S. No.	Year	Jammu City	Growth rate %	Jammu Distt	Growth rate %	Kathua	Growth rate %	Udham-pur	Growth rate %	Doda	Growth rate %	Rajouri	Growth rate %	Poonch	Growth rate %
(a) ATTA															
1.	1990-91	13081		5202	–	2060		5037		4841	–	1823		1401	–
2.	1991-92	16743	27.99	6303	21.16	2673	29.76	5725	13.66	5106	5.47	2000	9.71	1547	10.42
3.	1992-93	18587	19.2	6747	13.88	2740	15.33	5614	5.57	4738	–1.07	2179	9.33	1587	6.43
(b) WHEAT															
1.	1990-91			3850	–	3121		4671		16955	–	1534		2134	–
2.	1991-92			4409	14.52	2373	–23.97	8001	71.29	22116	30.43	1373	–10.49	2520	18.09
3.	1992-93			1060	47.53	3030	–1.47	8596	35.66	21895	13.64	2076	16.33	2009	–2.97
(c) RICE															
1.	1990-91	1991		1100	–	1233		5680		8962	–	1456		2523	–
2.	1991-92	3008	51.08	1511	37.36	1252	1.54	5265	–7.31	7484	–16.49	1408	–3.3	2153	–15.46
3.	1992-93	5183	61.34	1390	12.41	1746	19	5038	-5.82	6998	–11.63	2085	19.67	1887	–13.52
(d) SUGAR															
1.	1990-91	2125		4747	–	2171		2536		2395	–	1872		1303	–
2.	1991-92	1694	20.28	4775	0.6	2142	–1.33	2547	0.43	2365	–1.25	1916	2.35	1324	1.61
3.	1992-93	1729	9.8	4664	–0.88	2181	0.23	2338	–3.98	2288	–2.26	1925	2.83	1242	–2.37

Source: As per the Survey Conducted.

Table 1.11
District Wise Number of Fair-Price Shops Urban/Rural as on 31.03.93

S. No.	Name of District	Urban				Rural				Total			
		Govt.	Pvt.	Co-op	Total	Govt.	Pvt.	Co-op	Total	Govt.	Pvt.	Co-op	Total
1.	Jammu City	5	251	0	256	0	0	0	0	5	251	0	256
2.	Jammu Distt.	12	8	0	20	26	292	101	419	38	300	101	439
3.	Kathua	10	1	0	11	16	159	7	182	26	160	7	193
4.	Doda	8	6	0	14	38	149	9	196	46	155	9	210
5.	Rajouri	7	4	0	11	19	128	7	154	26	132	7	165
6.	Poonch	4	0	0	4	17	48	6	71	21	48	6	75
7.	Udhampur	17	1	0	18	28	130	38	196	45	131	38	214
	Total	63	271	0	334	144	906	168	1218	208	1177	168	1552

Source : As per the records of Directorate of Food & Supplies Department, Jammu

Excluding City.

Figure - 6

Import of Foodgrains

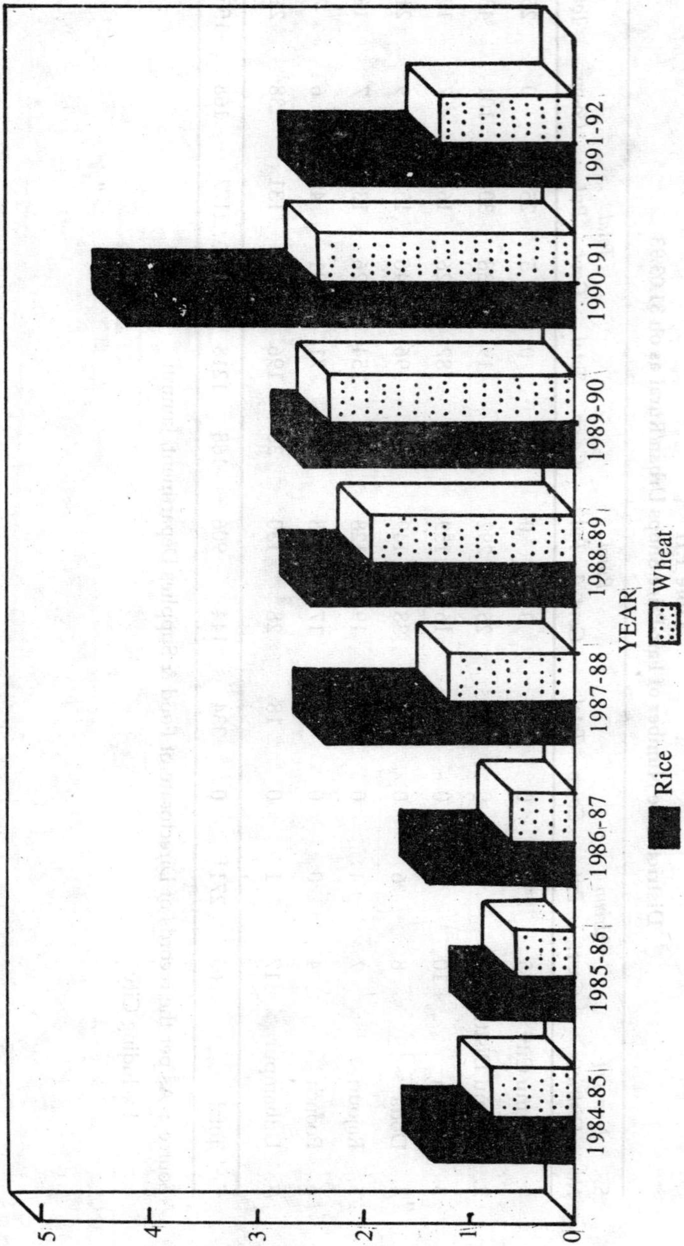

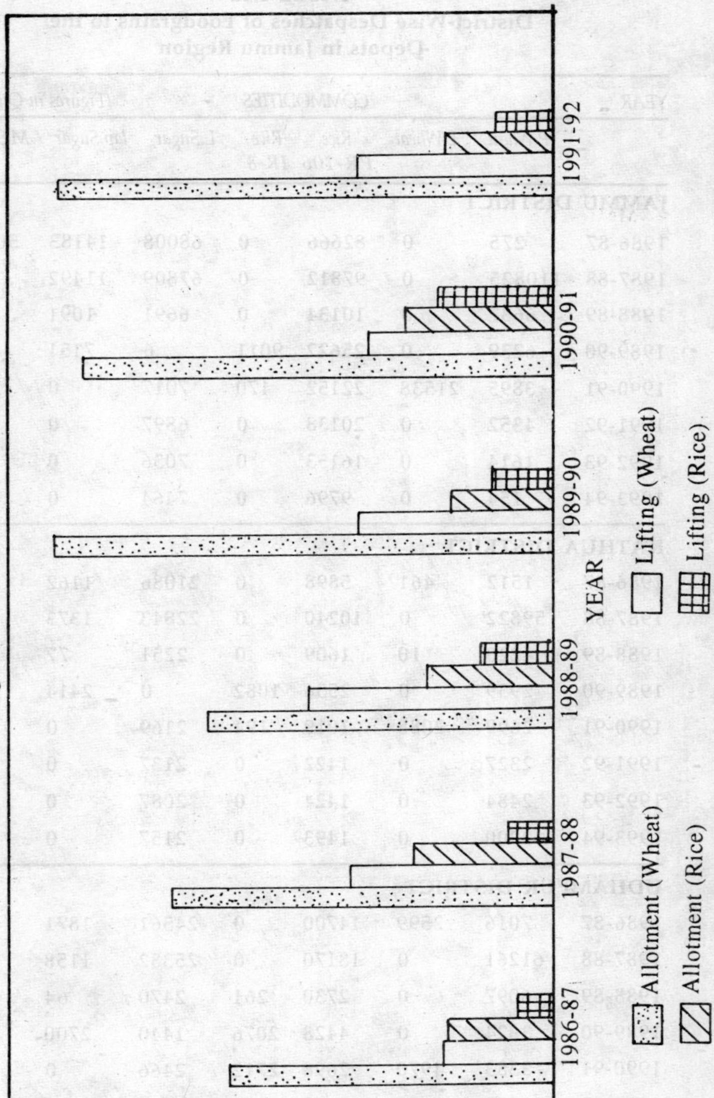

Figure - 7

Allotment & lifting of Wheat & Rice in Jammu Division

TABLE 1.12
District-Wise Despatches of Foodgrains to the Depots in Jammu Region

YEAR			*COMMODITIES*			*(Figures in Qtls)*		
	P.Wheat	*L.Wheat*	*Rice PR-106*	*Rice IR-8*	*L.Sugar*	*lap.Sugar*	*M.Sugar*	*Atta*
JAMMU DISTRICT								
1986-87	275	0	82666	0	68008	14183	505	64682
1987-88	110825	0	97812	0	67809	11492	0	19589
1988-89	6687	0	10134	0	6691	1091	0	29787
1989-90	6239	0	25622	9011	6	7151	3	0
1990-91	3895	21538	22152	470	7017	0	0	0
1991-92	4352	0	20138	0	6897	0	0	22366
1992-93	1614	0	16153	0	7036	0	0	27875
1993-94	154	0	9796	0	7464	0	0	25205
KATHUA DISTRICT								
1986-87	1512	461	5898	0	21086	1162	0	6290
1987-88	59822	0	10240	0	22843	1373	0	19363
1988-89	4220	10	1609	0	2251	77	0	2854
1989-90	2939	0	2556	1082	0	2414	0	0
1990-91	2699	2088	1019	194	2169	0	0	0
1991-92	2327	0	1422	0	2137	0	0	2463
1992-93	2484	0	1424	0	2087	0	0	2824
1993-94	2300	0	1493	0	2157	0	0	2846
UDHAMPUR DISTRICT								
1986-87	7016	2599	14700	0	24561	1871	0	8719
1987-88	61261	0	18170	0	25382	1158	0	28848
1988-89	6097	0	2730	261	2470	64	0	4662
1989-90	3624	0	4428	2076	1440	2700	0	0
1990-91	3383	4970	2698	2712	2466	0	0	0
1991-92	8556	0	4116	1848	2552	0	0	9687
1992-93	8319	0	4502	357	2386	0	0	5663
1993-94	11615	0	7292	3	2386	0	0	5457

YEAR			*COMMODITIES*			*(Figures in Qtls)*		
	P.Wheat	*L.Wheat*	*Rice PR-106*	*Rice IR-8*	*L.Sugar*	*lap.Sugar*	*M.Sugar*	*Atta*
POONCH DISTRICT								
1986-87	4763	8393	7037	0	13614	413	0	3201
1987-88	20039	0	6779	638	14684	156	0	12607
1988-89	3199	20	1698	18	1439	25	0	1534
1989-90	2391	0	1839	567	1222	1509	0	0
1990-91	2097	1424	541	2021	1306	0	0	0
1991-92	2547	0	1190	1126	1345	0	0	1480
1992-93	2533	0	1526	218	1145	0	0	1547
1993-94	1403	0	1408	310	1163	0	0	1389
RAJOURI DISTRICT								
1986-87	4319	3715	8174	0	20410	423	0	3849
1987-88	38458	0	6633	0	20670	306	0	13621
1988-89	3274	39	1262	99	2058	32	0	2159
1989-90	1427	96	1879	768	214	2161	0	0
1990-91	1560	1659	755	711	1892	0	0	0
1991-92	1324	0	915	570	1932	0	0	1881
1992-93	2223	1366	190	1704	0	0	0	2066
1993-94	2664	1937	490	1818	0	0	0	2250
DODA DISTRICT								
1986-87	51226	17074	21321	0	20761	480	0	9563
1987-88	167367	0	28931	209	23621	261	0	40483
1988-89	17514	40	4857	3854	2366	22	0	4980
1989-90	15796	0	5327	3818	3997	2764	0	0
1990-91	15495	5203	3220	6025	2447	0	0	0
1991-92	23258	0	3922	3798	2445	0	0	4670
1992-93	22428	0	6051	906	2360	0	0	4617
1993-94	22074	0	7427	749	2335	0	0	5424

Source : As per the Records of the Food & Supplies Department, Jammu.

Details of the district-wise despatches of foodgrains from the Food and Supplies Deptt. to the various urban and rural outlets, are shown in Table 1.12.

On an average, one fair price shop covers 2000 souls in rural areas and 1700 souls in urban areas as per the 1981 census on population basis.

6. REVAMPING OF PDS

With the change of the political executive at the national level in 1991, the Government accorded very high priority to the PDS and it was felt that the really vulnerable areas and people were not getting the desired benefits of PDS due to their disadvantageous geographic location, weak PDS infrastructure and low purchasing power. It was, therefore, decided that PDS should be reoriented for ensuring effective reach to the remotest and the most disadvantaged areas of the country, which also had maximum concentration of poor. Accordingly, around 1752 blocks, composed of tribal, hilly, drought prone and '**desertified**' areas, were identified and included in crash programme designated "Revamped PDS " or 'RPDS'. The plan of action included:

(i) A number of new FPSs to be opened so that physical access of beneficiaries is improved;

(ii) Special campaign to be mounted by the state governments to cancel the bogus, entitlement cards and to issue new cards to households found to be without them;

(iii) To progressively bring more and more FPS under the system of FPS doorstep delivery of PDS commodities;

(iv) Set up vigilance committees of local people with substantial representation of women for each FPS at the village level and also at higher levels;

(v) Improve the supply chain by constructing or hiring small intermediary godowns; and

(vi) Introduce additional commodities through FPS, in these areas.

An analysis of the implementation of RPDS has shown that during 1992-93, per capita allocation in RPDS areas was higher than other areas and whereas off-take (actual distribution) against allocation was only 73% in other areas it was 91% in RPDS areas. States were also moving towards the norm of 20 kg per family per month. The positive trend that emerges from the analysis is that the PDS, which was predominantly urban-biased till the mid 1980s has now been effectively targeted for the traditionally deficit areas covered by RPDS[14].

The plan schemes operated by the ministry were liberalised for assisting the states to take up construction of godowns in the Revamped PDS areas and for purchase of vans for use as mobile FPSs in those areas. Since the liberalisation of the scheme, Rs. 9.48 crore had been provided to the states for purchase of 170 vans. Similarly, under the godown construction/scheme, Rs 7.95 crore had been disbursed to the states and union territories for construction of 147 additional godowns for FPS items. To increase the availability of foodgrains for distribution in the RPDS areas, the Union Govt, had earmarked an additional two million tonnes per annum from the central pool[15].

The Central Issue Price (CIP) for such supply of foodgrains for these specific areas, as incented by the concerned Deputy Commissioner/District Magistrate/Collector would be on the specially subsidised rate i.e. Rs. 50/- less than the normal CIP w.e.f. 1.6.1992. The existing issue prices for ITDS supplies are as below:

Commodity	*CIP (under ITDP)*
Wheat	Rs.230/ per Qtl.
Rice (common)	Rs.327/ "
Rice (Fine)	Rs.387/ "
Rice (Superfine)	Rs.400/ "

The concerned authority has to furnish a certificate for the foodgrains lifted from the central pool under the scheme for having utilised the same in the identified blocks/areas at the time of lifting of foodgrains in the next round of allotments/supplies.

Monthly statement of total quantity issued area wise, block-wise and district-wise would be consolidated at the regional level by 20th of the following month and would be fed to the Zonal office/headquarters Latest by 25th of the following month and the quantities issued under specially subsidised rates tally as per the accounts[16].

7. NEED FOR REVAMPING PDS

It is on account of such factors that the liberalisers speak of the need to put a 'human face' or mask on the structural adjustment programmes. Revamping the PDS is another structural programme. In our country, the present regime has been emphasising quite stridently its commitments to strengthen the PDS. This is undoubtedly a very useful strategy and may lighten the burden of adjustment for the weaker sections. This is also in keeping with the basic thrust of the PDS which is a complementary element of the food economy which attempts to supply essential goods to the poorer sections at stable and affordable prices, particularly in view of the persistent inflationary pressures. During the later part of the 1980s, the need for strengthening the PDS increased on account of some additional factors. The adverse impact of rising food prices should be softened by making basic food items available to the identified needy in some fixed quantities at subsidised, fixed prices at regular, periodic intervals from authorised retail outlets, known as Fair Price Shops[17].

8. REVAMPED PDS IN JAMMU REGION

The said scheme has been introduced in 22 blocks of Jammu Region i.e. Doda District comprising of 14 blocks and 8 blocks of Udhampur District falling under Drought Prone Area Programme (DPAP) Under this scheme, foodgrains are being issued by FCI at price less by Rs. 50/-

per quintal from present ratio of the PDS out of which a benefit of Rs. 25/- per quintal goes to the consumers and remaining of Rs. 25/- per quintal is utilised for handling incidental charges. Accordingly, the rationees of these areas have been getting foodgrains at a cheaper rate by Rs. 25/- per quintal since June 1992.

In addition to foodgrains, other essential commodities are also being brought under the purview of the Revamped PDS as per details given below:

1. Pulses, 2. Tea, 3. Edible Oil, 4. Match box, 5. Iodized salt, 6. Soap, 7. Candles, 8. Note-books, 9. Clothes.

These commodities will be distributed through the co-operative societies on the price fixed by the National Agencies like National Co-operative Consumer Federation which arrange its procurement and supply through its societies. The first part of the scheme i.e. supply of foodgrains is being implemented through Directorate of Food and Supplies. The details of the grains utilised by District-wise since June 1992 under the scheme of RPDS in Jammu Region is given in Table 1.13.

Table 1.13
Utilization of Foodgrains under RPDS for the Years 1992 & 1993

(Figures in Qtls.)

Year	*Name of District*	*Utilization*	
		Wheat	*Rice*
1992	Doda	14391	3142
	Udhampur	5818	1642
1993	Doda	20005	6535
	Udhampur	12689	5645

The State Government has recommended Poonch, Rajouri, Guraze, Karnah, Machhil predominantly inhabited by Gujjars, Bakerwals and Dardas who have all been accorded Scheduled Tribe status by the Government of India for coverage under the Revamped PDS. The newly extended areas of the scheme will provide benefit to 7.09 lakh population in addition to the identified areas already covered

Table 1.14

Quantities of ration Dumped for Departmental Godowns/Outlets during 1992-93

(Figures in Qntls)

S. No.	Name of District	Area	Wheat 1991-92	Wheat 1992-93	Rice 1991-92	Rice 1992-93	Sugar 1991-92	Sugar 1992-93
1.	Doda	Paddar Duchham Chatru Gandoh MaruMangl	37035	0	8193	0	2629	0
2.	Udhampur	Gool Mahore Dasmasi Chasona Suggi	35600	22063	15900	8867	3605	3351
3.	Kathua	Bassi Lowang Duggar Mathur Dhuggaru	4700	5716	970	1430	560	742

Source : As per the Records of Food & Supplies Department, Jammu

by the scheme. The requirement of the extension areas in Jammu Region on the basis of 1991 projected population is given under:

S.No	*Name of the District*	*1991 Projected Population*	*Requirement of food Grains (fig in Qtls)*	
			Rice	*Wheat*
1.	Doda	4.17	4390	21140
2.	Poonch	2.92	3100	14832

In November 1991, the following quantities of ration dumped for the purpose in departmental godowns/outlets during the year 1992-93 are shown in Table 1.14.

RESEARCH METHODOLOGY

(a) Need of the study

In view of its crucial importance, the public distribution system has been extensively used in almost all parts of the country. Admittedly, the PDS is not a perfect system. Its short-comings are fairly well-known. However, while there has been much debate and criticism of the effectiveness and the desirability of continuing with the PDS in its present form, there have been very few studies on the operational aspects of the PDS. Consequently, suggestions for improvements of the PDS in its present format have mostly remained within the Government. The liberalisation of the Indian economy set in motion in the past few years, has generated renewed interest in social safety-net programmes such as PDS.

In the light of these facts, it becomes imperative to make an indepth study of the organisation and management of the public distribution system. Implementation has been one of the weakest links in our public policies. The study highlights several bottlenecks in the process of implementation of the PDS . It is not enough to have a well intentioned policy, it is equally important that such a policy should be backed by imaginative and sound organisational arrangements. This aspect comes out very well in the present study. It also brings out the need for rural coverage because a large number of people in these areas live below the poverty line.

Thus, this empirical study analyses the policy framework and the managerial aspects of the PDS at both the macro and micro levels. Further, it evaluates the working of the system at a micro level on the basis of consumer image and perception. The findings of the study by and large hold good at macro level also. The micro-level experiences of the operation of PDS have been discussed mainly to reveal the rural urban contrast in its effective operation.

(b) Objectives of the study

The present study has been undertaken with the following objectives in view:

(i) To examine the role of PDS in the Indian context in the light of publicly declared goal of protecting and augmenting the consumption levels of the economically vulnerable sections through the system;

(ii) To critically analyse and evaluate the operating efficiency of the PDS;

(iii) To examine the level of benefits that the rural and urban dwellers get from this system;

(iv) To analyse the consumption patterns in urban and rural areas to estimate the respective income elasticities in respect of food items;

(v) To assess the administrative ability of the State Government to run this system effectively; and

(vi) To suggest suitable measures in the light of the problems identified.

(c) Scope of the study

The present study is mainly confined to three types of subsistence items namely the food items viz; wheat flour, rice and sugar. The operational period of the study is 10 years ranging between 1983-1993.

(d) Hypotheses

Following are some of the hypotheses postulated in this study:

(i) The PDS of foodgrains in Jammu Region has been haphazard and has failed to maintain a steady supply to the consumers at reasonable prices.

(ii) The role of the FCI and the Food and Supplies Deptt. has not been satisfactory in distributing foodgrains and building up of the buffer stock for price stabilization.

(iii) The administrative machinery charged with the responsibility of running the PDS is ill-equipped to handle the system effectively.

(e) Sources of Data Collection: (Sample Plan)

(i) **Sample Unit**: The study is based on empirical data collected from both the organised and unorganised sectors directly engaged in the PDS. Under organised sector, the ration dealers and the agencies involved in the PDS have been undertaken. People availing the PDS facility have also been surveyed which constitute the unorganised sector for the purpose of the present study from both the urban as well as the rural areas.

(ii) **Sample Procedure**: The information and data for the present study have been obtained both through Primary and Secondary sources.

(a) *Primary Sources :* For this purpose, data has been collected through observation, questionnaires/ schedules, interviews and discussions with the persons having wide experience and Knowledge on the subject under investigation.

(b) *Secondary Sources :* For this purpose, data has been collected through books, journals, magazines, reports and review of literature of agencies engaged in the PDS in India in general and Jammu Region in particular.

(c) *Construction of questionnaire/schedule* : For the collection of Primary data, three schedules/ questionnaires have been drafted through extensive discussions with knowledgeable persons and after reviewing the literature on the subject. First questionnaire comprising the questions relating to consumer preference has been served to the persons availing this PDS facility. Second questionnaire has been served to different ration dealers and the third questionnaire has been for the officials of the agencies engaged in the overall managerial system of the PDS.

(iii) **Sample size** : For this purpose, 550 consumers have been surveyed and out of this, 500 have been found correct for analysis. Two Districts of Jammu Region have been taken, one with urban background and another with rural background i.e. the Jammu District and the other namely Udhampur District as the scheme of revamped PDS has been implemented in some rural areas of Udhampur District. Each district with one Tehsil and under Tehsil one block comprising of atleast one village have been covered. Again, 250 dealers have been selected from the same districts, out of which, 200 have been found correct for analysis. Almost hundred per cent of the official agencies responsible for this system in the Jammu Region have been contacted.

(iv) **Sample Media**: The respondents have been approached personally to get the first hand information. Mail and telephone systems have also been applied for the purpose.

(v) **Sample Design** : Both the urban and rural respondents/customers are taken for the study on the basis of multi-stage random sampling with stratification at the final stage by taking Income

as the stratifying variable. The dealers' selection for the purpose, has been made on the basis of systematic sampling procedure from the list of the dealers available from the Directorate of Food and Supplies Deptt. To get information from the agencies, simple random sampling method has been used. For the purpose of analysis, the respondents included in the sample are classified on the basis of their income, occupation and educational back ground. Table 1.15 shows the educational background, occupation and income of the respondents under study.

(vi) **Statistical Tools used** : In order to derive the substantial results from the information collected through questionnaires/schedules, various statistical tools like percentages, ranks, bar-diagrams, line-graphs and pie-diagrams have been used.

(vii) **Limitations of the study** : A study of this kind has its own limitations which condition the depth and quality of the study. But for these limitations, the quality of the study would have been better than what has been found possible.

Among the commodities covered in this study, only rice and wheat are procured by FCI in Jammu Region. Hence, the procurement problems faced by FCI related to wheat and rice only could be analysed. The distribution problems of rice, wheat and sugar are only studied as mostly these commodities are covered by PDS and purchased by the customers of the Region.

The findings of the survey regarding dealers' participation in the PDS are based on the discussion the researcher has had with the persons concerned and on the participant observation made by the researcher. Non-availability of the actual facts and figures has come in the way of the analysis of data at various points in the course of the study. However, the researcher has tried her best to operate even under such constraints.

Table 1.15

Educational Background, Income & Occupation of the Respondents who purchase/consumer ration items

S. No.	Occupation Educational Background	*Student*				*Service*				*Business*			
		Urban		*Rural*		*Urban*		*Rural*		*Urban*		*Rural*	
		%age	*No.*	*%age*	*No.*	*%age*	*No.*	*%age*	*No.*	*%age*	*No.*	*%age*	*No.*
1.	Illiterate							2	2.53	3	6.38	1	2.63
2.	Below Matric	2	3.12	3	6.52	10	8.33	9	11.39	5	10.64	3	7.89
3.	Matric	13	20.31	10	21.74	25	20.83	15	18.98	11	23.4	10	26.32
4.	Graduate	22	34.38	20	43.38	38	31.68	25	31.65	18	38.3	17	44.74
5.	P. Graduate	27	42.19	13	28.26	40	33.33	25	31.65	9	1915	7	18.42
6.	Professional Courses					7	5.83	3	3.8	1	2.13		
	Total	64	100	46	100	120	100	79	100	47	100	38	100

Table 1.15 (contd.)

Agriculturist				Profession				Any other				Total			
Urban		Rural		Urban		Rural		Urban		Rural		Urban		Rural	
No.	%age	No.	%age	No.	%age	No.	%age	No.	%age	No.	%age	No.	%age	No.	%age
		2	4.77									3	1.08	5	2.25
1	10	5	11.9					2	40	1	16.67	20	7.19	21	9.46
4	40	27	64.28					1	20	3	50	54	19.43	65	29.28
5	50	8	19.05	2	6.25	2	18.18	1	20	1	16.67	86	30.93	73	32.88
				12	37.5	4	36.36	1	20	1	16.67	89	32.02	50	22.53
				18	56.25	5	45.46					26	9.35	8	3.6
10	100	42	100	32	100	11	100	5	100	6	100	278	100	222	100

Table 1.15 (contd.)

S. No.	Educational Background	Income Group-I				Income Group-II				Income Group-III			
		Urban		Rural		Urban		Rural		Urban		Rural	
		No.	%age	No.	%age	No.	%age	No.	%age	No.	%age	No.	%age
1.	Illiterate			3	7.89	2	1.79					2	3.57
2.	Below Matric	2	8.7	3	7.89	15	13.39	13	15.66	4	4.4	3	5.36
3.	Matric	8	34.78	10	26.32	25	22.32	18	21.69	30	32.97	17	30.36
4.	Graduate	8	34.78	14	36.84	40	35.71	26	31.32	27	29.67	7	12.5
5.	P. Graduate	5	21.74	8	21.06	20	17.86	16	19.28	25	27.47	18	32.14
6.	Professional Courses					10	8.93	10	12.05	5	5.49	9	16.07
	Total	23	100	38	100	112	100	83	100	91	100	56	100

Table 1.15 (contd.)

Income Group-IV				*Total*			
Urban		*Rural*		*Urban*		*Rural*	
No.	%age	No.	%age	No.	%age	No.	%age
		1	2.23	2	0.72	6	2.7
1	1.92			22	7.91	19	8.56
9	17.31	2	4.44	72	25.9	47	21.17
18	34.61	19	42.22	93	33.45	66	29.73
24	46.16	23	51.11	74	26.62	65	29.28
				15	5.4	19	8.56
52	100	45	100	278	100	222	100

Source : As per the survey Conducted

Note : Urban Respondents = 278
Rural Respondents = 222
Total Respondents = 500

REFERENCES

1. Gupta, Arvind., "Public Distribution of Foodgrains in India" Monograph no. 69. Centre for Management in Agriculture, Indian Institute of Management, Ahmedabad, 1977, p. 83.
2. Suryanarayana, G., "*Public Distribution System in India*", 1985, p. 15.
3. Nawani. N.P., "*Towards Food for All-Ideas for A New PDS*", 1995, p. 65.
4. Ojha, Ghanshyam Das., "*Organisation and Management of PDS*", 1987, p. 14.
5. Nawani, N.P., "*Towards Food for All-Ideas for a New PDS*", 1995, p. 66.
6. Venugopal, K.R., "*Deliverance from Hunger*" *(The PDS in India)*, 1992, p. 82-83.
7. Nawani, N.P., "*Towards Food for All-Ideas for a New PDS*", 1995, p. 67.
8. Venugopal, K.R., "*Deliverance from Hunger*" (The PDS in India), 1992. p. 9.
9. Suryanarayana, G., "*Public Distribution System in India*", 1985, p. 13.
10. Nawani, N.P., "*Towards Food for All-Ideas for a New PDS*", 1995, p. 3.
11. Khurana Rakesh et.al., : "*PDS-Evoluation, Evaluation & Prospects*", p. 200.
12. The Economic Times, 19th Jan, p. 8.
13. Nawani N.P ; '*Towards Food for All-Ideas for a new PDS*', 1995, p. 69-70
14. Ministry of Civil Supplies, Public Distribution & Consumer Affairs, 1993.
15. Daily Excelsior, 27th June, 1995, p. 5.
16. As per the Records of the Food Corporation of India, Jammu.
17. Kabra, K.N & Rao, E.K., "*The PDS & the Liberalisation*" "Productivity", Vol. 33, July-Sept, 1992, p. 230.

Chapter–2

Review of Literature

The PDS has been functioning for more than four decades now, if its predecessor, the rationing system is left aside. It's greatest achievement lies in preventing more families in India. As recently as the 1987 drought which has been considered one of the worst in the century, the PDS helped the country to overcome it with dignity and effectiveness. The PDS also, no doubt, played a great role by making available rice and wheat at the fixed prices to consumers in all nooks and corners of the country, thereby preventing the spectre of famine in any part of the country. This distribution network also supplied grains for the "food for work" programmes taken up on a large scale to fight the drought.

The present chapter is devoted to a review of earlier studies on the public distribution in India in order to identify gaps in research, if any, and in helping to formulate methodology of the present study.

The study made by Bhatia (1970)[1] has covered the aspects of India's food problem and price control and mainly dealt with the food policy without laying adequate emphasis on the problem of PDS. He considered that the broad objectives of food policy were intended to safeguard the interests of low income consumers, in availability as well as in price and to ensure that producers received reasonable prices with an adequate incentive for increasing production.

Raj Krishna's (1970)[2] study on the government operations in foodgrains presented some normative models and the study was based only on the secondary data. He suggested that the beneficiaries of the distribution system could be arrived at by deducting from the total population (1) the number of income -tax assesses and (2) cultivator households multiplied by five which was the average size of the family.

An evaluation of fair price shops was made by V.B. Singh (1973)[3] adopting the empirical method but the study was confined to the functioning of public distribution system in an urban area only. The shop owners complained about the low income from the source. Two alternatives were envisaged under the circumstances; either the shopkeepers engaged themselves in malpractices to augment their income or they were honest enough to lead the life of austerity. Both these situations needed correction from the Government view point.

Gulati and Krishnan (1975)[4] tried to outline a scheme to cover all the people under poverty, both from the rural and the urban areas, on a permanent basis with an assured supply of 100.80 kgs. of grains per person per annum. The quantity required to feed such a large number of people came to about 30 million tonnes in 1973. The estimates of foodgrains made in this study were found to be too-large to the extent that they could not be mobilized either from internal production or from imports or from both.

Gupta (1977)[5] studied the effectiveness of PDS. He examined the price stability achieved through the operation of PDS using econometric models and found that the quantities required to meet it would be very much higher than what could be generated internally through procurement. The additional requirements were several times of the total foodgrains distributed through the PDS. Based on certain assumptions and secondary data projected foodgrain requirements for PDS upto 1980 for the entire country. Such projections were assumed to help policy makers in their procurement efforts.

George (1979)[6] analysed the impact of foodgrain issues through PDS on the consumption levels of the poorer sections and on the interest of both the producers and consumers of the State of Kerala. The consumption of rice was found to be lower in the absence of rationing for all the consumers. But the low-income consumer groups were the worst affected. The excess of income accrued to the producers in the absence of PDS was lower than the additional expenses borne by the consumers. In the short-run, the objective of the protection of the consumption level of the low income groups could be met better through grain supplies, through PDS than the income transfers.

Similar study has been attempted by Gavan and Chander Shekhra (1979)[7] for Sri Lanka. Based on consumer survey data, they examined utilisation of ration by different economic groups in rural, urban and estate areas and concluded that a high proportion of total cereals consumed was obtained through the PDS by all income groups. In terms of cash equivalent, the value of subsidy was 16 per cent of total income for the tenth percentile of the population. Such incremental income, according to this study, enabled the consumers to increase the consumption of different products. However, the identification of target groups for percolating the benefit of the public distribution system had not been attempted in the above study.

Subba Rao (1980)[8] attempted to estimate food requirement for the state of Andhra Pradesh under certain assumptions. In the rural areas, PDS covered : agricultural labour population' and families of workers engaged in household industries. For urban areas, the entire urban population excluding the income-tax assessees households were to be included in the PDS. While working out these estimates, he assumed a supply level of 12 Ozs. (340gms) per consumption unit and concluded that the Andhra Pradesh was not a surplus state and people in the deficit districts were made to depend on the open market.

Garg (1980)[9] studied the operational aspects of the Food Corporation of India and described it as a study in policies and practices of PDS without covering any aspects of distribution of goods procured and organisational and managerial aspects of PDS.

Bapna (1980)[10] described the management structure of the PDS in India. Policy formulation, fixing of objectives, strategy for procurement and distribution of foodgrains and other essential commodities were discussed in detail in the study. The PDS as an alternative approach to private trade was not justified because the available evidence suggested that private trade in foodgrains was quite competitive. Its existence could be justified if it generated more competition in the market. Due to very high fluctuations in foodgrains production, the PDS was fully justified for its buffer stock operations. In this case, the elaborate distribution and procurement system were not necessary. The findings have also shown that the PDS had been used as a major instrument for the supply of foodgrains in urban areas. A study in Lucknow city during 1968-69 indicated that with the exception of card holder in the highest income group, about one half of the card-holders in every income group purchased wheat from the ration shops. The highest income group accounted for only three per cent of the total card holders and only one-fourth of this group purchased wheat from the FPS.

Narayana (1982)[11] in his study 'Demand Supply Gap and Public Distribution of Foodgrains in India' aimed at analysing the demand supply gap in foodgrains over time stated and suggested the ways to alleviate the gap. The study was based upon published data. A variety of methods had been applied to pursue various objectives. The demand had been estimated through the regression analysis. The NSS household consumption data of 27th Round had been used for the purpose. Supply functions were estimated through the regression analysis using the time-series data published by the Ministry of Agriculture, Government of India. It was found that demand-supply gap could be zero, positive or negative for different states at the same time. A model for the correction of the demand-supply gap was suggested. Wide variation was seen in the consumption of rice, wheat and total cereals not only among the states but also among the different income groups within a state. Among the factors influencing the demand for foodgrains, population, income, price, family size and price of the substitutes were found important. Thus, the findings helped in formulating a viable and realistic operational policy for the PDS. The need for such a policy would increasingly be felt in future as the PDS had to play an important role.

Suryanarayana (1985)[12] attempted to analyse the working of PDS in Andhra Pradesh and Vishakhapatnam in the study 'Public Distribution in India'. The consumption patterns, income elasticities for selected commodities, impact of rationing on consumption in terms of net income benefits and a critical evaluation of the working of FPSs and the PDS had been analysed by the researcher. The theory of Dual Market Mechanism was applied to measure the benefits due to public distribution. The exact magnitudes of benefits would be known by taking into account the difference between open market price and fair price and by multiplying the difference with the quantum distributed through FPSs. Consumption elasticities were also calculated to examine the effect of income changes on consumption of the selected commodities. Growth rates of linear, exponential and compound types were calculated for rice, wheat and sugar with regard to their distribution. The sampling procedure followed for the selection of households and for the collection of data from the urban, rural and tribal areas, two stage stratified random sampling design was used in the study by canvassing a questionnaire designed for the purpose. The findings of the study had shown that the economic status of the respondents in urban, rural and tribal areas had not been very encouraging. The patterns of consumption of essential commodities revealed that consumption was generally higher among rural consumers except in case of sugar which was consumed more by an urban consumer. This was testified also by the figures of per capita consumption worked out on the basis of the field data. The purchasing pattern revealed that FPSs' were meeting about 38 per cent of the wheat requirements, 35 per cent of the rice requirements and 86 per cent of sugar requirements. As regards the priority to specific categories in respect of allotment of FPSs no single category emerged as popular among most of the respondents. The various suggestions were also incorporated to improve the overall working of this system.

The study 'Organisation and Management of Public Distribution System' by Dr. Ghanshyam Das Ojha (1987)[13] based on the empirical research, examined several individual case studies of agencies which were involved in the PDS. This volume analysed the policy framework and the organisational structure of the PDS at both the macro and micro levels. The data was collected from the consumers of FPSs/ration shops functioning in urban and rural areas. The purposive random sampling method was adopted for the selection of the respondents. Besides consumer respondents, data was also collected from 20 Private fair price shops with the help of a schedule. Thus, the study attempted to focus on the aspects related to the organisation and management of PDS from the point of view of the cross section of the society, Government and its agencies and others concerned with the functioning of the PDS. The analysis highlighted three major points—firstly the distributive mechanism was unscientific; secondly, it was not tailored to suit the needs of the weaker sections in general and the rural poor in particular and thirdly, there were unhealthy practices by various sections resulting in the large scale breakdown of the instrument of PDS. The common short comings such as irregular release of quotas, wide gap between demand and supply, absence of salesmanship, discourteous behaviour, pilferages caused by the vested interests, interference of the influential persons and lumpen elements, non-viable nature of the FPSs, strained relations between the consumers and the dealers and the unfavourable disposition towards the PDS were found to be widely prevalent in running these FPSs. Thus, the micro analysis lended support to the major findings of the study.

Patil (1988)[14] focused on the rural public distribution and the co-operatives by analysing its strategic role in the PDS in this country. Consumer co-operatives were organised among the industrial and mining workers, employees of railways, post and telegraphs and other public and private industrial estates. About 3,600 such establishments out of total 5,100 had organised consumer co-operative stores. It was also observed that in the villages, the service co-operatives as well as marketing co-operatives themselves took the responsibility of the distribution of essential consumer articles. The volume of the retail trade handled by the co-operatives during 1984-85 was of the order of Rs. 750 crores. The findings showed that inspite of massive financial assistance, the performance of Gram Panchayat Level societies in distributing the consumer goods in rural Assam was not satisfactory. The performance of the Mini Super Bazar in Andhra Pradesh was also not very satisfactory because of want of trained manpower, experience in the retail trade and financial difficulties. The idea of co-operativisation of the distribution trade in rural Maharashtra got frustrated before it actually came into practice. So, the author was of the opinion that the only effective way to help the rural consumer was by way of organising the co-operative consumer stores to supply not merely the controlled articles but all the basic consumer goods.

Verma and Prasad (1990)[15] examined the public distribution system and its operational efficiency both in micro and macro settings by drawing samples both from urban as well as rural areas of Bihar. The micro level experiences of the operation of PDS had been discussed mainly to reveal the rural-urban contrast in its effective operation. The analysis of the data collected by the researchers showed that the PDS with its operations had not been able to fulfil its purpose of protecting vulnerable population of the society from inflationary pressure. The food basket of the lower quarter of the population had not been even partly filled by this system. The process of price stabilisation regulation was to be initiated by the policy makers taking into consideration the various implications of the measures taken on the food front. The Indian food rationing was primarily concerned with an equitable distribution of available foodgrains. It meant the imposition of a ceiling on consumption in order to equate supply with demand in Bihar in particular and at all India level in general. Four different systems of rationing namely statutory, Non-statutory or informal (rural) controlled distribution and market stabilisation through relief and fair price shops were suggested to make this system more effective.

An indepth study was carried out by Shenoi[16] (1990) under the special scheme of PDS in ITDP blocks of Ranchi and Palamau districts of Bihar State. The specific objectives of the study undertaken, were :

1. To critically evaluate the special scheme of distribution of foodgrains in the ITPS blocks.
2. To analyse the role of various agencies involved in the scheme
3. To examine the working of the FPSs and the needs of the people in the ITPS blocks; and
4. To make suitable suggestions for improving the effectiveness of this special scheme in the tribal areas.

To understand the working of the FPSs and the needs of the tribal people, a detailed survey of 30 FPSs and of about 225 ration card holders from eight such blocks were contacted.

The findings showed that the cardholders didn't lift their full requirement of foodgrains from the FPS because lifting was permitted only twice a month and they didn't have enough money to meet their requirements. 25 per cent of the respondents complained of irregularity in the supply of commodities and the functioning of the FPSs, improper weighing of commodities and inadequate supply of kerosene and non-refund of small changes.

Mahendra Dev (1991)[17] et.al made an attempt to verify severe criticisms against the PDS in India on the grounds that it was urban biased and it benefitted by and large the middle and upper income groups. To evaluate the validity of these criticisms, the latest available National Sample Survey Data on 'Utilisation of PDS' was used. To collect the data, 47,827 rural households and 27,736 urban households were contacted. Four different criterias i.e. rural sector's share in total PDS purchase, relative dependence on the PDS given by ratio of PDS purchase to total purchases, PDS quantity purchased per capita and PDS quantity purchased per market dependent were taken into consideration to examine whether PDS was urban-biased or not. The results had shown that the nature of bias varied depending upon the commodity in question and criterion used. The data at the All-India level showed that the PDS was not favouring the middle or richer groups. More or less, all the population groups depended uniformly to the same extent on the PDS with respect to all commodities in rural areas, even though there were slight variations.

Kacker (1991)[18] examined the current status and the role of the distribution function in the context of developing countries in Asia and Africa. This study incorporated views of panel members who examined distribution systems in India, China and other developing countries in Africa. Different distribution strategies were found to be effective in the overall Public Distribution system. Statistical Data on distribution was collected on regular basis by appropriate Government agencies. In India, basic data on distribution was collected by the Population Census Economic Survey of India and a host of co-operative and private industry organisations. The findings revealed that the marketing systems were being used as a political tool to control and channelise resources from farmers to government. In India, small independent firms of retailers, wholesalers, agents and brokers were predominant in the distributive trade.

Koshy (1991)[19] focused on one of the major concerns raised about the efficiency of the PDS, i.e. the extent of diversion of the stock of commodities from the FPSs to the open market. This study was carried out in Kerala, where the PDS was perceived to be relatively better developed and more effective when compared with others states in India. Factual information was obtained regarding the quantity of commodities actually purchased by the card holders based on the entries in their respective ration cards and quantity sold to the same card holders for the corresponding period as recorded in the card register maintained by the fair price shopkeepers. Thé sampling procedure followed was a two-step process. The collection of data was based on the quantity of rice purchased from the FPS during the month of observation from a sample of 805 card holders drawn on the random basis from all districts of the state. The important aspects emerged from the analysis of the data showed that out of the total quantity recorded by the FPSs as sold to the bonafide consumers, only 69 per cent reached them and in all probability, the remaining 31 per cent get diverted to the open or black market. Another important point was that the excess quantity recorded by the FPSs as sold to the consumers was significantly more in case of the ration card holders belonging to the higher income groups.

Kabra and Rao (1992)[20] examined the impact of the liberalised policy regime on the scheme of providing inflation-insulated supplies of essential food items through the PDS. The paper also explored the adverse consequences of the liberalised economic policies and the scope of setting them right by strengthening and redesigning the PDS. The hypothesis that the better off, more organised and those living in the urban areas in the backward blocks were likely to corner much of the benefits available under the RPDS, was put to test during the study. The results showed that the study had not taken into account the pattern of regional variations and the concentration of poor inhabitants. Some limitations of these steps had been brought out covering different factors and reducing the effectiveness of the PDS by the low utilisation of its supplies. It was also found that the loopholes in the administrative design of the PDS operations resulted in leakages of the meagre supplies to unintended channels, non-availability of entitlements with FPS dealer in collusion with civil supply authorities, irregular supplies, inferior quality of grains supply and restrictions on drawals according to the consumers' capacity and convenience.

The study 'The Public Distribution System in a Designated Hill Area of North Western Uttar Pradesh' by Anil C Ittyerah (1992)[21] made an attempt to look into the functioning of the PDS and identification of the priorities from among the various measures, suggested as a part of the revamping scheme, on the basis of actual field level observations. The survey was conducted by two teams, first to study the functioning of the two fair price shops in the area, while the other to assess consumers' behaviour the degree of consumer access and utilisation of PDS facilities as well as the general perceptions of the beneficiaries regarding the functioning of the PDS at Laxmangarh. Turning to the lifting of individual commodities, it was found that with the exception of sugar, both cereal and kerosene oil lifting was very low. The dealers were of the opinion that both access and viability should considerably be improved by introducing a system of regular shop floor delivery and the introduction of additional commodities. The surveyed households were unanimous in their assertion that PDS played a critical role in holding down the price line for essential commodities and the system should be strengthened by widening the commodity coverage by including items such as pulses, mustard oil, vanaspati, soap and tea. The general awareness regarding the machinery for the registering and redressal of grievances, was low among consumers. Keeping in view the various issues and suggestions that emerged in the course of field survey, different measures that deserved top priority in any attempt to revamp and strengthen the PDS in identified hill blocks, were needed to be emphasised.

Venugopal (1992)[22] studied on the topic 'Deliverance from Hunger—The Public Distribution System in India' in which he discovered that some states, which did not produce enough foodgrains, had a far better record of providing food for the poor than states which had a surplus. Various issues like the intensity of hunger in rural poor households, the financial constraints involved in the rational use of foodgrains in rural wage employment programmes, reorientation of the PDS to serve only the poor and the need for involving the community in food management were also discussed. Seven villages of the four districts of Andhra Pradesh were taken for survey to know the functioning of the rice scheme. The study revealed certain serious drawbacks in the scheme. The results showed that a very substantial percentage of the beneficiaries, who were daily wage earners, were unable to buy their entire monthly entitlement. It was also observed during the study that the scheme had also changed the complexion of Andhra Pradesh PDS and achieved certain other unanticipated gains for the agricultural labour class and other poor in the rural areas.

Sanathanan (1992)[23] conducted a study on PDS in the rural areas of Kerala. The study found that the number of ration cards served in the rural areas of the state was six times more than that in the urban areas. The study also stated that inspite of 156 per cent increase in FPS, till 1990 the issues like non-availability of food items, insufficient norms and malpractices associated with FPS were the disturbing facts of PDS in the state. The study was conducted with a specific objective to examine if the FPSs, as an integral part of the PDS, had succeeded in meeting the requirements of the rural population. The major focus of the study was on the responses of the 120 beneficiary households selected by simple random sampling method from Mangattidom village of Kannur District of Kerala. The information was collected with the help of an interview schedule and it was found that 70 per cent of the respondents were satisfied with the location of FPS and the distance from their residence to FPS and the rest expressed dissatisfaction. An overwhelming majority of the respondents held the view that the quality of sugar and edible oil supplied under the PDS, was good.

Howes and Jha (1992)[24] presented the paper on 'Urban Bias in Indian Public Distribution System' and evaluated the single definition of the word 'bias' used in the study. The PDS was said to be urban biased in respect of a given variable, if it was found that, in relation to that variable, the average urban dweller gained more from the PDS than the average rural dweller. Three different variables were used to measure bias. Comparisons were conducted over rural and urban levels of PDS quantities consumed, implicit subsidies and accessibility. Any household with a registered residential address was entitled to be covered by the scheme. The main data source was the 42nd Round of the National Sample Survey (NSS), carried out in Sarvekshana (GOI, 1990). This survey collected information on the consumption of rationed goods at the household level, possibly for the first time in India, at least nation-wide. With over 70,000 households surveyed, the data source was potentially a rich one. Supply data from 1978 showed a massive urban bias across all states and union territories. Consumption data from 1986-87 showed a mixed picture though with an urban bias on average. The second measure of bias presented showed that the 'economic value' of the PDS depended on the difference between the market and ration prices as well as on quantities consumed. The final measure of bias i.e. accessibility of ration shops, suggested that the rural dwellers were disadvantaged in relation to their urban counterparts only to the extent that shops were on an average at more distance. Crowding and coverage were of similar magnitude in both the urban and the rural areas.

Jha (1992)[25] examined the purchasing power of the poorer section particularly the Scheduled Tribes knowledged to be the poorest among the poor groups in India. The study was carried out in Bihar where the population of tribals is 8.31 per cent of the total population. The tribals are compelled to rely mostly on agriculture and live mainly on produces like the vegetables, rice and some coarse grains such as maize, millets etc. Till recently they had little liking for wheat. Hence, they were not dependent on PDS for their food supply. Under the ITDP Scheme, the quantum of foodgrains to be distributed, was fixed at 12 kgs of wheat and 4 kgs. of rice. But the quantity of rice was revised later and reduced to 1kg per adult per month. The study also revealed the tremendous change in the food habits of tribals. The tribal consumers complained about general shortages of concessional foodgrains at the Fair Price Shops. To make the system more effective it was suggested that the SFCs' sales units located in 'haat' (weekly markets) centres should also be ensured so that the sales centers were not closed on 'haat' days. Mobile vans with adequate stocks and staff should be pressed into service. There was an urgent need for an effective enforcement machinery to ensure that the commodities were distributed to the right persons, in right quantity and at the right price.

Kabra and Ittyerah (1992)[26] worked on the study based on the one hand, on primary data obtained through a sample survey covering the whole country and on the other, on an analysis of secondary data about different aspects of the PDS. It examined the evolution and operation of its overall design as a policy and a programme as an integral part of food economy of India taking into account its regional specifications. Its emphasis was on both the various socio-economic variables and the administrative arrangements for regularly delivering fixed quantities of certain essential commodities at inflation-insulated prices. Through an analysis of the interaction of these factors in their micro and macro aspects, it attempted to bring out the dynamics of the PDS and place it against the background of the various objectives sought to be achieved through this state intervention in the market processes. In the context of twin questions of target group orientation and viability of FPS, the study evolved an integrated package of policy and administrative measures for increasing the effectiveness of the PDS as a component of the minimum needs programme for the poor. The process of improving the viability of the FPS should go hand in hand with the process of serving more consumers and serving them better.

The study 'Public Distribution system : Access of the Poor—A Case Study of a Jhuggi Jhompri Cluster' (1993)[27] was carried out by the Deptt. of Administrative Reforms & Public Grievances. It was based upon a survey of two jhuggi jhompri settlements in the Union Territory of Delhi. The study was designed to reveal insights into the manner in which the Public Distribution System serves the needs of the poor. To ascertain that the residents of Jhuggi-Jhompri cluster were poor, the study team carried out a survey of jhuggi jhompri dwellers in west Delhi, Pilikothi and Santadham. Besides ascertaining incomes of the households, questions were asked about the literacy level, the number of school going children, asset structure, type of fuel used, possession of consumer durables so that some cross verification of reported income level could be made. Till the end of 1989, there were 1.39 lakh food cards issued to Jhuggi dwellers, a reflection of adhoc concessions to selected mature Jhuggi settlements. The survey revealed that 97 per cent of the households got their food cards made directly from the circle office. The juggi dwellers were unable to utilise the PDS because they lacked the purchasing power to draw the allocated quantity of ration at one time in a fortnight or month. It was because, the earnings of the jhuggi dwellers were so meagre that they were not capable of accumulating money for buying rations out of their daily, erratic incomes. It was found that the quantity of cereals issued to the dwellers by FPS was inadequate to meet their needs. There was disparity between the entitlement and the allocation norms. Allocation of foodstuffs was being made at a much lower rate than the entitlement per unit.

Suryanarayana and Geetha (1993)[28] examined about critical issues of reorganising the PDS. This paper had made an attempt to examine some of the questions arising from the issues under consideration to be specific, it attempted to answer the following questions:

(i) What had been the objectives of the PDS and had they changed in successive five-years Plans?

(ii) Was there any disparity in the state-level distribution of the PDS?

(iii) If there had been proper targeting of the PDS only towards the people below the poverty line?

The system of food controls to be maintained had to be related to the needs of the urban and other highly deficit areas. The study was based on data on total public distribution of foodgrains, obtained both from central and State governments, taken from the various issues of the Bulletin on food statistics. The authors had reviewed the objectives of food policy pursued in different Five-Year Plans examined inter-state PDS disparities and their implications for the current on-going PDS reforms. Time series data was used to examine the question under consideration with the help of rigorous statistical tests. The Centre allotted 19.11 million tonnes (in 1990-91) and 24.72 million tonnes (in 1991-92) of rice and wheat for the states, the offtake was only 14.94 million tonnes and 18.77 million tonnes respectively. Thus, PDS revamping was not merely a question of targeting but also involved the creation of the necessary infrastructure, like storage facilities and distribution network, particularly in states like Bihar and Orissa.

Nawani (1995)[29] tried to analyse the role of the PDS in achieving the objective of food security in the study entitled 'Towards Food For All—Idea for a New PDS'. The global situation relating to food security and a historical perspective of food management in India were described in detail in the study. The scenario of production and availability of foodgrains and dynamic relations between poverty, purchasing power and consumption of foodgrains were also examined with a view to improve the effectiveness of the PDS rather than on alternative models for ensuring food security.

For the field study, Chamoli and Uttarkashi districts were selected within Garhwal Himalayas, for a sample survey of fair price shops and PDS beneficiaries on a random basis out of the four hill districts. The information was collected from the District Magistrates regarding population etc, in the selected districts. The overall food and nutrition availability appeared to be much better in Uttarkashi as compared to Chamoli. Assuming an average family in these hills to consist of four adults and two minors, the requirement of cereals on the basis of nutritional norm of 167.8 kg per capita per annum came to approximately 70 kg per month. The supply of cereals from the PDS to such a family came out to be only 24 kg or 34 per cent of requirements in Chamoli and 19 kg. or 27 per cent of the requirements in Uttarkashi district. These statistics revealed that the PDS was playing only a marginal role in meeting the nutritional requirements of an average family.

From the foregoing review, it is indicated that most of the studies conducted in India have not dealt with the costs and political feasibility of targeting of PDS and have also reported a high percentage of leakages in the event of targeting. The main weakness in the PDS, i.e. not reaching the vulnerable section of the society for whom it is actually made, effectively stems from the universality of the PDS coverage. Further, there are the studies done earlier to the introduction of the National Production-cum-Distribution Scheme.

Based on the aforesaid review, the present study is an addition to the current literature on the subject as it endeveours to study the major objectives of the PDS i.e. adequacy of rural coverage, management of the fair price shops under the scheme, consumers perception and the image of the PDS at work, administrative and the managerial aspects of the PDS at the Central and State level to assess their ability to run this system effectively and to suggest suitable measures in the light of the problems identified.

Thus the study proposes to examine the major objectives of the PDS and their actual impact. In other words, the present study seeks to examine the gap between the promise and performance of the PDS.

REFERENCES

1. Bhatia, B.M., 'India's Food Problem and Policy Since Independence', Somaiya Publications, Bombay, 1970.
2. Krishna, Raj., 'Government Operations in Foodgrains', The Economic and Political Weekly, Sept. 1976.
3. Singh, V.B., 'Evaluation of Fair Price Shops', Oxford and IBH Publishing Co., New Delhi, 1973.
4. Gulati, S.C., 'The Pattern of Income Distribution in India' A Review in "Poverty & Income Distribution in India", Edited by Srinivasan, T.N., 'Statistical Publishing Society', Calcutta, 1975.
5. Gupta, Arvind., "Public Distribution of Foodgrains in India, Monograph No. 69, Centre for Management in Agriculture, Indian Institute of Management, Ahmedabad, 1977.
6. George, P.S., 'Public Distribution of Foodgrains in Kerala' (Income Distribution, Implication and Effectiveness) Research Report 7, International Food Policy Research Institute, Washington, March, 1979.
7. Gavan, J.D., & Chandershekhra, I.S., " The impact of food grain Distribution on Food Consumption and Welfare in Sri Lanka ", Research Report 13, IFPRI, Washington, Dec. 1979.
8. Subba Rao, K., 'What is A surplus State? Public Distribution of Rice in Andhra Pradesh', Arth Vijnana, vol. XXII No. I, March 1980.
9. Garg, Vipin., 'Food Corporation of India, State in Foodgrains Trade in India'—A study of policies & practices of PDS, Birla Institute of Scientific Research, New Delhi, 1980.
10. Bapna, S.L., 'Food Security through the PDS' The Indian Experience, 1980.
11. Narayana, S., 'Demand-Supply Gap and Public Distribution of Foodgrains in India', Himalaya Publishing House, New Delhi, 1982.
12. Suryanarayana, G., 'PDS in India', Chugh Publications, Allahabad, 1985.
13. Ojha, Ghanshyam Das., 'Organisation and Management of PDS', Mittal Publications, Delhi, 1987.
14. Patil, M.B., 'Rural Public Distribution and the Co-operatives', Indian Journal of Public Administration, Vol. XXVI No. II Jan-March, 1988.
15. Verma, B.N. and Prasad, Samiti., 'PDS—A theoretical Perspective', Uppal Publications, 1990.

16. Shenoi, G.V., 'Management of PDS in Tribal Areas : A Study of Ranchi and Palamau in Bihar', The Indian Journal of Public Administration, Vol XXXVI, No 1, Jan-March 1990.

17. Mahendra Dev, S. and Suryanarayana , M.H., 'Is PDS Urban Biased & Pro-rich?' Economic & Political Weekly, Vol XXVI, No. 41, Oct—1991.

18. Kacker, Madhav and et.al., A paper presented in 3rd International conference on Marketing and Development, New Delhi—Jan. 1991.

19. Koshy, Abraham., 'Malfunctioning of PDS', An Empirical Analysis' Vikalpa, Vol.16, Jan-March, 1991.

20. Kabra K.N. & Rao, E.K., 'The PDS & the Liberalisation', 'Productivity, Vol 33, No. 2, July-Sept. 1992.

21. Ittyerah, Anil C., 'The PDS in a Designated Hill Area in North-Western U.P.', 'Indian Journal of Commerce', Vol No. XLV, Part III, Sept-1992.

22. Venugopal, K.R., 'Deliverance From Hunger', Sage Publications, 1992.

23. Velluva, Sanathanan, 'PDS in Rural Area—A Case Study', 'Yojana', March-1992.

24. Howes, Stephen and Jha, Shikha., 'Urban bias in Indian PDS', Economic & Political Weekly, A Sameeksha Trust Publication Vol. XXVII, May-1992.

25. Jha, Jai Prakash., 'Food Distribution in Tribal Areas', 'Yojana' Vol. 36. No 8, May 1992.

26. Kabra K. N. & Ittyerah, Anil C., 'The PDS in India', Eastern Books , New Delhi, 1992.

27. Deptt. of Administrative Reforms & Public Grievances, 'PDS-Access of the Poor—A case-study of a Jhuggi Jhompri Cluster', 'A Journal of Administrative Reforms', 'Management-in Govt,' Vol. XXIV, No-4 Jan-March 1993.

28. Geetha, S. & Suryanarayana, M.H., 'Revamping PDS : Some Issues & Implications', 'Economic & Political Weekly', A Sameeksha Trust Publication, Vol XXVIII, No 41 Oct. 1993.

29. Nawani, N.P., 'Towards Food For All—Ideas For A new PDS', Ministry of Information & Broadcasting, Government of India, New Delhi- 1995.

Chapter–3

The Administration and the Organisation of the PDS

I. MANAGEMENT OF THE PDS

There is an increasing awareness among the practising administrators in India of the need for introducing modern management culture in the realm of public administration to make administration more active, sensitive and responsive. This is of particular value in that it paves the way for greater professionalism in public administration and also facilitates development of an infrastructure for a dynamic system of organisation, designed to make the administration more efficient and humane.[1] Effectiveness of the PDS and its capacity to serve the vulnerable sections depend, in addition to the macro aspects connected with the national food policy, on a large number of policy decisions regarding the operational and organisational aspects of the PDS. There issues are largely a matter of decision-making by the state governments.[2]

In the present study, an attempt is made to analyse the organisation and management of PDS in Jammu Region. The term 'Organisation' in this study relates to the organisational arrangements/structure at Central and State level with a special emphasis on the organisational set up of PDS at the district level and below . The term 'Management' refers to the managerial aspects of the fair price shops which play an

Figure 9
THE PUBLIC DISTRIBUTION SYSTEM: A SIMPLE MODEL

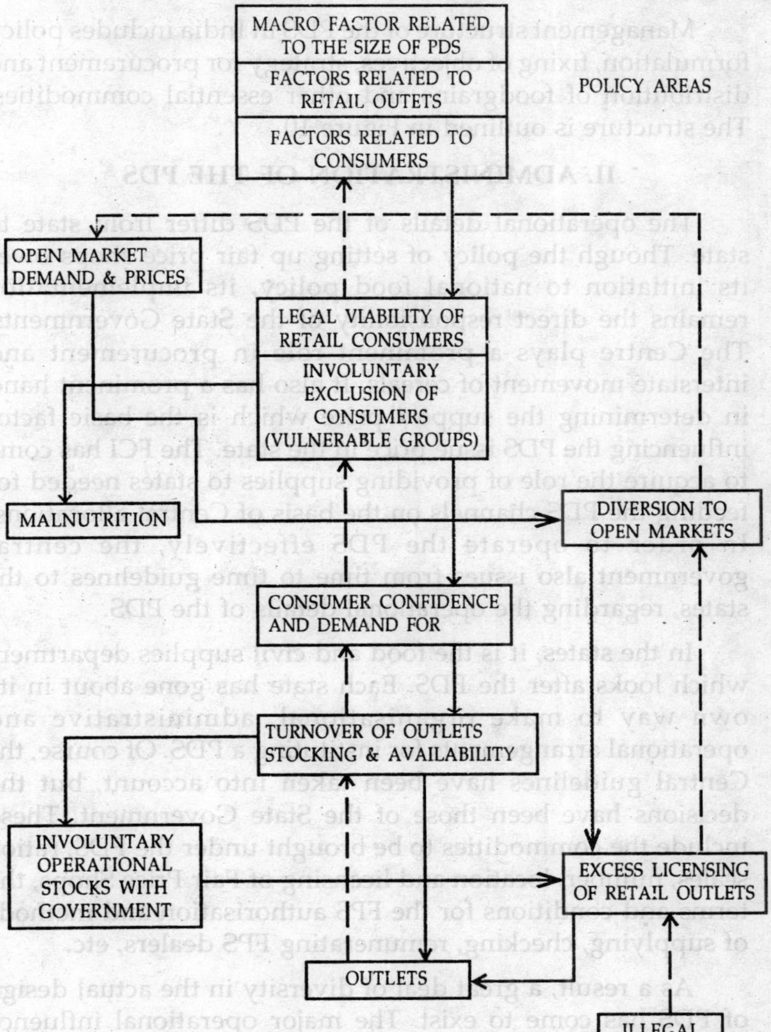

NOTE:—
DOMINANT EFFECTS ⟶
FEEDBACK EFFECTS — — ⟶

important role in the retail distribution of essential commodities.[3]

Management structure of the PDS in India includes policy formulation, fixing of objectives, strategy for procurement and distribution of foodgrains and other essential commodities. The structure is outlined in Figure 10

II. ADMINISTRATION OF THE PDS

The operational details of the PDS differ from state to state. Though the policy of setting up fair price shops owes its initiation to national food policy, its implementation remains the direct responsibility of the State Governments. The Centre plays a prominent role in procurement and interstate movement of cereals. It also has a prominent hand in determining the support price which is the basic factor influencing the PDS issue price in the state. The FCI has come to acquire the role of providing supplies to states needed for feeding the PDS channels on the basis of Central allocations. In order to operate the PDS effectively, the central government also issues from time to time guidelines to the states, regarding the operational details of the PDS.

In the states, it is the food and civil supplies department which looks after the PDS. Each state has gone about in its own way to make organisational, administrative and operational arrangements for instituting a PDS. Of course, the Central guidelines have been taken into account, but the decisions have been those of the State Government. These include the commodities to be brought under the PDS, ration scales, number, location and licensing of Fair Price Shops, the terms and conditions for the FPS authorisation and methods of supplying, checking, remunerating FPS dealers, etc.

As a result, a great deal of diversity in the actual design of PDS has come to exist. The major operational influence can probably be seen in two crucial matters. Firstly, the allocation of wheat, rice, sugar, edible oil, kerosene, controlled cloth, etc., to the states. Secondly, the determination of the central ex-godown price for the centrally supplied

Figure 10

ORGANISATIONAL DESIGN OF THE PDS IN INDIA

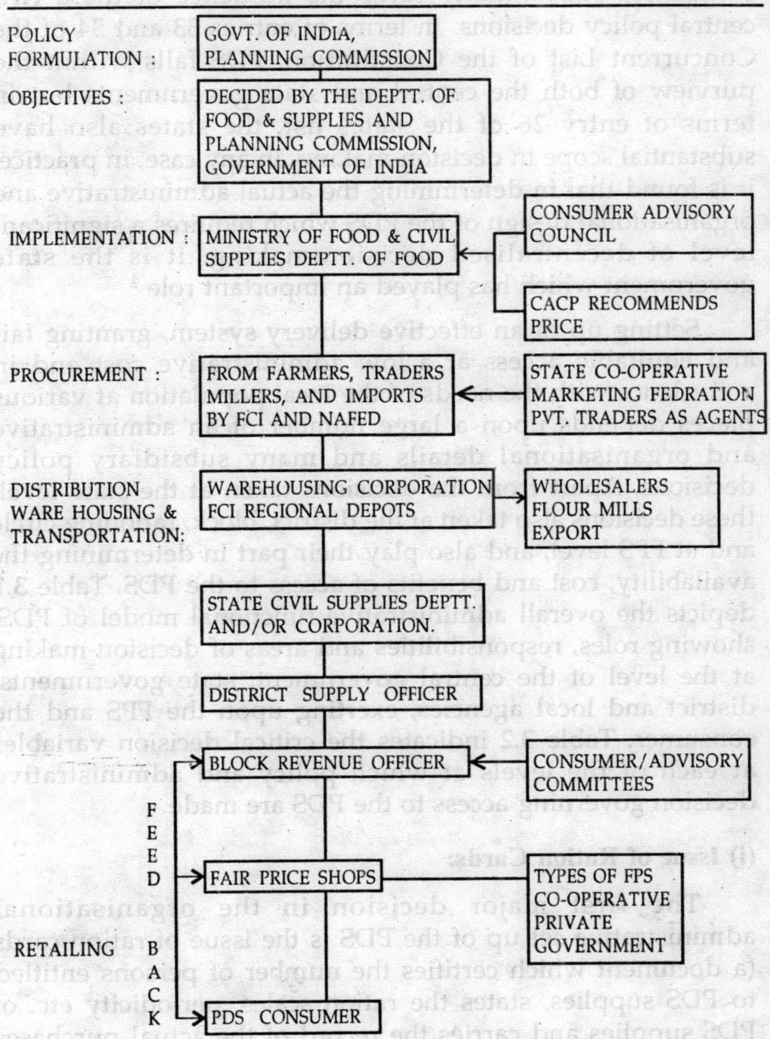

commodities. The ration scale granted by a state, their regularity and the final issue price charged from the consumers substantially carry the influence of these two central policy decisions. In terms of entries 33 and 34 of the Concurrent List of the Constitution, PDS falls within the purview of both the central and state governments but in terms of entry 26 of the states list, the states also have substantial scope in decision-making. In any case, in practice, it is found that in determining the actual administrative and organisational design of the PDS which requires a significant level of decentralised decision-making, it is the state government which has played an important role.[4]

Setting up of an effective delivery system, granting fair and equitable access at a low administrative cost and in accordance with the needs of the local population at various places depends upon a large number of an administrative and organisational details and many subsidiary policy decisions. Apart from the decisions taken at the state level, these decisions also taken at the district, block, rationing circle and at FPS level, and also play their part in determining the availability, cost and benefits of access to the PDS. Table 3.1 depicts the overall administrative functional model of PDS, showing roles, responsibilities and areas of decision-making at the level of the central government, state governments, district and local agencies, exerting upon the FPS and the consumer. Table 3.2 indicates the critical decision variables at each of the levels at which policy and administrative decision governing access to the PDS are made.

(i) Issue of Ration Cards:

The first major decision in the organisational administrative set up of the PDS is the issue of ration cards (a document which certifies the number of persons entitled to PDS supplies, states the ration scales, periodicity etc. of PDS supplies and carries the record of the actual purchases of these supplies). This also involves a decision about whom to grant access to the PDS, on what terms and conditions and to what extent.

Table 3.1
The Administrative Functional Framework.

CENTRAL GOVERNMENT	1. Obtaining supplies, procurement & imports; 2. Procurement price, issue prices to states, subsidies; 3. Guidelines to states on the design of PDS; 4. Allotments to states.
STATE GOVERNMENTS	1. Receipts of Central allocation; 2. Procurement in the state; 3. Purchases from other states; 4. Warehousing; 5. Determination of: *(i)* Consumer issue price; *(ii)* Commodity coverage; *(iii)* Ration scales; *(iv)* Rules for issue of ration cards; FPS licence; *(v)* Profit Margins to FPS; *(vi)* Periodicity of sale 6. Allotments to District & Transport Arrangements.
DISTRICT OR LOCAL AGENCIES	1. Lifting stocks; warehousing; 2. Issue of ration cards; 3. Licensing of FPS dealers 4. Arranging/Ensuring lifting by FPS dealers 5. Enforcement , Inspection, Vigilance.

TABLE 3.2
Important Decisions at Various Levels

Level	Decisions
CENTRE	1. Commodity coverage; 2. Total PDS supplies, procurement by imports/Exports + inventories; 3. Size of covered population: Exclusions; 4. Nature of PDS support-total or supplementary; 5. Preferential treatment to area or population group; 6. Difference between open market price by PDS issue price; and 7. Size of subsidy.
STATES	1. Matching of supplies with needs by intra-state procurement; 2. Adequate and well-dispersed warehousing; 3. Capacity to buy from other states; 4. Inclusion of additional goods; 5. Appropriation of issue price in relation to open market price; 6. Commodity coverage; 7. Periodicity; 8. Ration scale 9. Cost by Ease of getting ration card; 10. Location and behaviour of FPS; 11. Adequacy and profit margin; 12. Adequacy and regularity of allotment; 13. Public, private or co-operative transport of stocks to FPS; and 14. Transport charges, zoning for the purpose.

Table 3.2 Contd.

DISTRICT & LOCAL AGENCIES	1. Delivery to FPS of assured quality and quantity. 2. Proper storage by FPS; 3. Cost & case of betting; 4. Variation in State Government determined scales; 5. Ensuring regularity in lifting of stocks by FPS for round the year availability; 6. Need for reserve stocks; Rate to state deliveries to FPS; and 7. Government monitoring of stocking & Sales performance of FPS.

The process of making an application for the ration card and the process of verification, the time-taken for issuing the ration card, the conditions which have to be satisfied for the issue of ration card and the procedure for recommendation or verification, and the practice of charging a certain fee for the ration card differ from state to state. Generally, one has to make an application by filling in a form and then a food inspector visits the household for verification and after sometime, the applicant has to go to the civil supplies office for collecting the ration card. This generally involves three visits to civil supplies office. Not only does this take a lot of time, but most often poor people find it very difficult to obtain the ration card. At times, their ration card gets issued to someone else by various kinds of manipulation or simple administrative lapses. In states, with rather irregular supply of PDS goods, some people do not find it worth while to pay the fees or taxes and spend time for obtaining a ration card. If issuing of ration card can be considered the gateway for obtaining access to the PDS supply, it can be said that the gateway is not easily accessible to the poor people living in rural areas and away from the administrative headquarters of the food and civil supplies department so also, is the case with the people in urban areas who live in slums or who are temporary migrant workers.

In some states, all the members of a family are not included in the ration cards. Informal instructions are given for restricting the number of family members particularly in rural areas. Two patterns of rationing, namely statutory and modified, are operating while issuing the ration cards. In the statutory rationing areas, everyone is given a ration card and is entitled to obtain a uniform scale of ration supplies. This enables people to stagger their purchases according to the availability of cash at different points of time during a week. In the modified rationing areas, the state civil supplies authorities are in the process of issuing ration cards to every family. In this area, the ration scales are lower than they are in the statutory rationing areas. In the modified rationing areas, there is a scheme for excluding certain families from the supplies of cereals on the basis of the size of their land holdings while other families are given differentiated cereal ration entitlement on the basis of landholdings.[5]

In the State of Jammu & Kashmir, PDS is being operated with differentiation among three groups in terms of ration scale and issue prices. In the first group are included urban families whose family incomes are Rs. 600/- p.m. They are charged what is called landed cost price. In the second group are included the urban families, whose incomes are less than Rs. 600/- p.m. They are charged lower price than the landed cost for the ration supplies. The low income families are not charged a low price uniformly for the entire quantity of ration supplies they are entitled to, but they are charged different prices for various quantities according to a scheme of gradation.

As against different prices charged from the urban low income and high income families, in the rural areas, all the families are charged "landed cost price", irrespective of their economic status. In addition to non-subsidised price, the families residing in rural areas are also given lower ration scale. In addition to this formal arrangement, there also takes place another informal discrimination against the rural families whereby the entire strength of a rural family is not included in the ration cards. In this way, entitled ration supply for the rural households is reduced. This is a source of discrimination which is some what arbitrary and different families come to be treated differently on the basis of their capacity to deal with the administrative machinery. The discrimination against rural families, particularly the poor families, is carried further by making them obtain their PDS supplies from two different sources. If it is taken into account the fact that a rural family has generally to travel a longer distance to reach the fair price shop and that the supplies of the PDS quantities are generally more irregular in the rural areas, it may be concluded that there is a manifold discrimination against the rural poor in the scheme of PDS as it operates in the state.[6] Thus, it can be seen that in terms of ration issuing criteria, some states have introduced a certain degree of differentiation in their PDS towards different groups of population. In Jammu & Kashmir, there is a certain order of discrimination between urban and rural population and again in the urban areas, between high and low income groups. This discrimination is in terms of price charged for the PDS supplies for cereals though the price differences are small. By and large, in the entire country, more or less a universal coverage of consumers for the supply of cereals has been given with some minor exceptions.

(ii) Procedure For Issuing Ration Cards:

The procedure for issuing ration cards generally follows different patterns for the urban and the rural areas. In the urban areas, one has to make an application to the civil supplies authorities for obtaining a ration card. In the rural areas, ration cards are issued by village Panchayat or village Patwaris or some equivalent institution or agency. The procedure in the urban areas involves some inherent discrimination against the poor illiterate, homeless, slum-dwellers and temporary, migrant workers because they cannot satisfy all the formalities and requirements like that of a permanent residential address. Similarly, those who live at a relatively longer distance from the ration card issuing authorities, or those who live in inaccessible areas, have to incur a relatively greater real monetary cost for applying for, and obtaining ration cards. While some people may not obtain ration cards or may not succeed in doing so, some manage to obtain ration cards that may be called 'bogus ration cards'. One fairly common practice is to inflate the number of family members by including the names of servants, benamis, relatives, dogs, pets, etc. In many cases, the purpose of obtaining bogus ration cards is the desire on the part of the FPS dealers to divert the PDS supplies. For this purpose, the FPS dealer in connivance with the functionaries of civil supplies department, get bogus ration cards made.

(iii) Commodity Coverage:

The utility and significance of the PDS are greatly dependent on the commodities which are supplied under it at fixed price and in desired quantities. Partly on account of the importance of cereals in the consumption basket and partly on account of the national food policy, major cereals are covered in PDS by all the states. Wheat and rice, the main cereals produced and consumed in the country are supplied everywhere under the PDS. The wheat and the rice account for over 95 percent of the PDS supplies of cereals and share of coarse grains rarely exceed 5 percent, generally remaining around one to three percent.

In the urban pockets predominantly inhabited by the industrial working class, construction labour and workers employed in the informal sectors, there is a distinct preference for wheat flour (Atta) as compared to wheat.

The preference for atta is largely because it is convenient to consume specially by the working people who cannot afford the time and effort of cleaning and milling of the wheat supplied through the PDS. In J&K, where whole wheat flour is distributed especially in the urban areas of Jammu Region, it has a significant impact on the consumption of the poor and the offtake of Atta is substantially higher than that of wheat in the neighbouring regions.

Apart from cereals, certain other commodities are also included under the PDS. Important among these are sugar, edible oil, kerosene oil and controlled cloth. Sugar is the universal and most regularly supplied PDS commodity. This is also the commodity sold through out the country at a uniform PDS price.

(iv) Ration Scales:

Another important aspect of the PDS is the determination of ration scales or entitlements for every adult and child for the commodities supplied through the PDS channels. A large number of considerations influence the determination of the entitlement per family or per person. The ration scales even for the commodities, which are supplied under PDS all over the country, like wheat, rice, sugar, edible oils, differ widely among and even within various states. The ration scale for rice and wheat would differ among the states on basis of the fact whether rice or wheat constitute the staple food of the majority of the people in a particular state. Similarly, an informal rationing or PDS may not provide ration entitlement equal to the full demand or need of the people.

A decision to fix ration scale will have to be based on certain assumptions about the demand and need concerning the average consumption pattern in a particular area. In addition to the considerations operating on the demand side, many factors regarding supply, availability, production patterns and overall surplus or deficit position of the commodities concerned will also exercise their influence. It is well-known that the deficit states place their demands with the central Government for obtaining the PDS supplies. The ration scales prevalent in various states may be expected to differ from each other, depending on whether the states are surplus' or 'deficit' in cereals.[7]

(v) Periodicity of Purchases:

The PDS is not only a system of predetermined, fixed price, fixed quantity, supply of some selected essential goods but also a system with a certain fixed periodicity of purchases. The PDS permits only a fixed periodicity of purchases. One can buy on one's ration card a given amount of PDS goods, at a fixed price from a predetermined source of supply at an interval of given periodicity. It means that the frequency of purchases and the size of each purchases from the PDS are determined by a set of rules and regulations. These rules impose certain restrictions on the consumers, though it is also essential to fix the periodicity of purchases in order to plan supplies from the supplying agency to the FPS.

Most states have gone in for a monthly system of periodicity, i.e., permitted one purchase every month, because it simplifies the task of the FPS dealers. It also helps the consumers, to the extent that he has to make only one visit to the FPS. However, it would be unrealistic to assume that the majority of intended beneficiaries of the PDS have a regular monthly income. A large number of urban casual workers, landless agricultural workers, tenants, small landholders, several artisans in rural and urban areas, self-employed persons and urban informal sector workers and many such persons do not have a regular income flow. Their income flows are irregular and uncertain, having a changing periodicity.

Given the income level, housing situation and availability of utensils for storage of monthly cereal requirements it is unrealistic that a large number of intended beneficiaries of the PDS would be in a position to buy their monthly cereal requirements for the whole month in one single instalment. Thus, the questions of periodicity, lapsing of entitlement and lumping together of purchases of all PDS commodities, therefore, are no mere routine administrative matters. These have a clearly identifiable hand in the granting or denial of the extent of access to the PDS, particularly to the poorer sections of the society.

(vi) PDS Issue Price:

The Centre Issue Price (CIP) is related to the support

price announced by the Central Government The determination of support price is a complicated task and is influenced by many considerations relating to national food policy. Following from the CIP, ex-godown prices are fixed for making supplies to the state governments. This includes, transport and administrative Overheads incurred by the Food Corporation of India. On the basis of the exgodown price and taking into account transport, handling, storage and interest charges and the margins given to the FPS dealers, the issue prices to consumers are fixed.[8]

The price at the PDS outlet is kept at a level lower than the open market prices and the difference between the price at which FCI issues to states and economic cost to FCI, is borne by the Government out of the food subsidy budget.[9] The difference between the Central Issue Price and State Retail Issue Price varies quite substantially among the various states.

Currently, issue prices for the PDS are Rs. 402 for wheat, Rs. 537, Rs. 617 and Rs. 648 per quintal for common, fine and superfine rice varieties respectively.[10] The subsidy paid to the FCI has been going up and up, inspite of the widening gap between the procurement prices and the issue prices of foodgrains from the Government godowns. The PDS has been distributing annually, on an average, 16 million tonnes of foodgrains, which suffice for a population of only 10 crores, on average consumption rate of 160 kg per capita per year. The gap between the PDS and the open market prices is so low that people are finding it easy to buy foodgrains in the open market. The present differential between the prices at the fair price shops and the open market shops is less than Re 1/- a kg. But even if it assumes to be Rs. 1.25 a kg., it can enable 10 crore genuinely poor persons to buy their foodgrains from the open markets by paying them cash. Thus, the govt can get away by paying only Rs. 2,000 crores, instead of Rs. 5,250 crores provided for in the 1995-96 budget as food subsidy. With Rs. 5,250 crores relief can be provided to more than 26 crore persons. The common rice, issued from the central godowns at the uniform price of Rs. 5,37 a kg. which is already heavily subsidised by the Central Government is being sold in different parts of the country to different categories of consumers, at least at a dozen different prices ranging from Rs. 2. to Rs. 6.60 a kg.[11]

Table 3.3
Rationed Price of Food Items

S.No.	*Food Items*	*Price (per qtls)*
In Jannu Region (in Urban Areas)		(In Rupees)
1.	Wheat	437
2.	Atta	452
3.	Rice PR-106	680
In Jammu Region (in Rural Areas)		
4.	Rice PR-106	725
5.	Rice IR-8	605
Under RPDS		
6.	Wheat	377
7.	Atta	388
At the FPS		
8.	Atta	467
9.	Rice PR-106	673
10.	Rice IR-8	512

Source : As per the Information received from the Directorate of Food & Supplies Deptt. Jammu.

The existence of the PDS as a constant supply arrangement in order to protect the purchasing power of the poor consumers in the frame-work of a national incentive price policy for the growers of the cereals requires that a certain minimum price difference between the PDS and open market prices be maintained. This is an important policy issue which has clear implications for the organisational and administrative aspects of the PDS from the points of reducing costs of handling and for coordination with other state agencies and departments in order to avoid taxing PDS supplies meant for the poor.

(vii) Quality of PDS Supplies:

The users of the PDS often complain about the poor quality of the cereals and at times, of sugar, supplied by the FPS. In certain areas, the criticism of the quality of the PDS supplied commodities is very strident. However, it appears that the reasons for poor quality are rarely properly understood.

The macro level design of the PDS policy which makes the PDS a component of a dual market and its relatively small size has some identifiable consequences for the quality of wheat, rice etc. procured by the public agencies for supply through the PDS channels. Uniform procurement prices for fair average quality of grains are announced and no premium is paid for superior qualities. It is quite natural that the open market bulk buyers are attracted towards superior qualities, while the public procurement agencies end up buying the poorer grades. The procured grains further deteriorate owing to poor warehousing. Thus, it is to be expected that the PDS supplies are relatively lower grades of quality, compared to the private, uncontrolled market, which is able to procure better qualities.[12]

The inherent difficulty of the PDS to acquire control over better qualities, is made still more difficult by poor storage and care in transit and made still worse by the storage and handling conditions at the FPS. The possibilities of adulteration or substitution of government supplied quantities by others may be added to the poor quality of grains.

The quality conscious better off sections are inclined to opt out of the PDS supplies of cereals on the grounds of quality of cereals they would like to consume. However, there is little reason to provide only inferior qualities of inflation-insulated supplies of cereals to the relatively worse-off, when bulk-cleaned, properly stored, graded and prepackaged supplies with guaranteed correct weightment can be provided under the PDS in order to make it serve its objectives better. This quality factor would not only improve offtake from the

PDS, but also serve its nutritional goals as well. It would mean improving the poor man's access to cereals, both qualitatively and quantitatively.

It is seen that though formal exclusion may be limited, there are some other factors which may informally restrict access to the PDS. Such factors have important bearing on who benefits from the PDS and to what extent. It is the decisions concerning them which determine the effectiveness of the PDS, i.e., who benefits from it, at what and whose cost, to what extent and how much in conformity with the expressed or implicit policy goals. A large number of arrangements concerning FPS also contribute to the same direction. These factors bearing access to the PDS have been only to a limited extent consciously and carefully recognised in designing the PDS operations.

(III) TARGETISATION OF THE PDS OR REVAMPING PDS

The country like India has to have PDS as a safety net till income of all the households have risen to such levels that each of them is able to afford adequate quantities of foodgrains, to enable each member of the household to lead an active and healthy life. The country is going to take some more time to reach that situation and PDS as a safety net for poor has to continue. The relevance of PDS is even more today when the economy is being liberalised and globalised, as during this transition period certain households would not be able to cope up unless assisted by the government. There is no option but to identify those households which require such assistance for extending the facility of subsidised foodgrains to them. Maintaining or improving the welfare of the poor requires either increasing or targeting the present untargeted safety nets.

Subsidising Poor House-holds:

One of the objectives of the PDS is to provide low basic foodstuffs to the poor and increasing their nutritional status. The food-subsidy in India accounts for about Rs. 5,200 crore in the revised budget 1993-94 and Rs. 4,000 crore in the budget estimate for 1994-95. Part of this subsidy is also used for maintaining buffer stocks. The PDS seems to be the main answer for the problems created by the liberalisation programmes.[13] Government has to devise a system or mechanism through which such subsidy will flow to the poor households in a more accountable manner. Some of the well-known systems to targetiبe the food subsidy are:

(i) Dual Price System:

The PDS is based on this system except that, certain commodities at lower prices than market, are available to everybody and not necessarily to the poor. The price at the PDS outlet is kept at a level lower than the open market prices and difference between the price at which FCI issues to states and economic cost to FCI is borne by the Government out of the food subsidy budget. The system has ideally provides the lower retail (subsidised) price and thereby a transfer in income only to the poor households, which have either been identified on the basis of their incomes and may live in compact identified geographical areas which are inhabited uniformly by poor households.

(ii) Food For Work:

This system looks very attractive as it seeks to combine two social objectives—providing direct (wage) employment to poor households and improving their access to food by distributing subsidised foodgrains to them against a part of their wages. It is also self targeting, since no non-poor will like to do the manual work on the projects undertaken under this programme. Therefore, there is no scope for diversion of subsidy to the non-poor.

(iii) Subsidising Poor People's Food :

Because of the diversity in food habits and cereals available for consumption, such a programme of displacing the Present PDS may not be acceptable either to the PDS beneficiaries or to the political leadership.[14]

(iv) Identifying Target Families For PDS:

Identifying the target families is a major hurdle in the entire process of targetization of the PDS for the poor. It is necessary to identify the needy families in the best possible manner before any step towards targetisation can be taken. One of the basic problems is to determine and perceive a criteria for determination of poverty and then to physically identify the poor households that qualify to be covered. This can be done either by an "income" method or by an "exclusion" method.

Income Method: A threshold income, which can buy required amount of food for each member of the family, can be worked out and all families having incomes higher than that can be taken out of the PDS. However, assessing incomes of millions of households, especially in the rural areas and in unorganised sectors, is an extremely difficult and complicated task whether the identification is based on self reporting of incomes or assessment by Government functionaries, inaccuracies, wilful or otherwise, are likely to remain.

Exclusion Method: In view of the enormous practical problems in implementing identification of target families based on incomes, more or less similar objectives can be achieved by excluding from the targeted PDS, certain categories whose incomes would surely be above the prescribed threshold limit. There is no doubt that this method is expected to be substantially less cumbersome than physical assessment of incomes of millions and millions of poor. It may afford more flexibility to state Governments also one of the problems that more and more categories may have to be added in the list of excluded categories till one arrives at the desired size of population which can be sustained by the targeted PDS, with the foodgrains and subsidy that the states would receive. On balance of considerations, exclusion method appears to be the most appropriate for Indian conditions.[15]

Categories to be excluded from the PDS : Some of the categories that could be considered for exclusion are given below:

(a) Income Tax payers.

(b) Property Tax payers may be above a certain limit so that families having small dwellings are not excluded just on the basis of Property Tax.

(c) Persons owning establishments registered under shops and Establishment Act and Sales Tax Regulations. In the rural areas, those having regular shops with pucca construction can also be excluded.

(d) Salaried employees in public and private sector, receiving salaries higher than that received by a Grade IV employee in the Central Government.

(e) Professionals registered as Doctors, Engineers, Lawyers, Chartered Accountants, Architects, etc.

(f) Persons owning industrial units, using power on commercial rates including small scale units, as also those owing rice shellers, atta chakkies, oil expellers, etc., in the rural areas.

(g) Persons owning agricultural/horticultural holdings above a certain limit which can be different for irrigated and non-irrigated lands.[16]

IV. QUANTITY TO BE DISTRIBUTED AND SUBSIDY TO BE PROVIDED FOR TARGETED PDS

It is observed from the data available in the Ministry of Food that, if a nine year period is taken from 1984-85 to 1992-93, the annual average procurement of foodgrains (rice & wheat) for the central pool comes to 179 lakh tons. It will, therefore, be more practical to take on a commitment of assured distribution of a quantity of not less than 150 lakh tons at substantially reduced prices to poor households. Of course, the allocation pattern of this quantity will necessarily be different from what it is presently.

As regards subsidy required for a reformed PDS targeted to only poor households, there could be a number of alternatives which could lead to different amounts of subsidy required. The present system is highly unsatisfactory as it is actually Minimum Support Price driven, the increase in procurement cost, generally being neutralized by corresponding increase in the issue price at which FCI delivers PDS grains to be allowed some additional subsidy which was Rs. 0.50 per kg. till recently and has now been raised to Rs. 1.00 per kg. In such a system, there is no room for protecting the poor households from unbearable inflation. The main constraint with such targeting is administrative feasibility and the costs involved in targeting. Even if the so called, "creamy layer" is removed, the food subsidy level may not come down significantly. The PDS, though, is not the only answer to the problems caused by marketisation, because it can help only those who have purchasing power.

The State Government of Jammu & Kashmir has pleaded for continued coverage of the PDS to the entire population of the state irrespective of any income slab including the income tax payers in view of its peculiar geographical and economical conditions. The projected population of 1991 in the state is approximately 78 lakh.[17]

V. AGENCIES INVOLVED AND THEIR FUNCTIONS IN THE PDS IN THE JAMMU REGION

The Government of India, State Governments and a number of other agencies are involved in arranging procurement, movement, storage and distribution of different commodities which are supplied under the PDS. At the Central level, the department of food provides policy directions and general supervision and the Food Corporation of India handles the procurement and the sales prices of foodgrains from the central pool are determined by the central Government on the basis of recommendations from the Agricultural Prices Commission and the views expressed by the National Development council.

Some of the State Corporations act as agents of the FCI for procurement and internal distribution. Many State Governments have their own Food and Civil Supplies Departments. In some areas, Producer Co-operative Societies are involved in procurement and Consumer Co-operatives are involved in distribution.

In certain cases, the FCI acts as the wholesale agent for both procurement and distribution. At the state level, foodgrains are distributed through licensed retail shops known as Fair Price Shops or ration shops. The extent of coverage of Fair Price Shops and eligibility for purchase from these shops are determined by the State Governments. The transport charges, commission to the retailers and prices of the foodgrains at the wholesale and retail levels are fixed by the State Government.

So, FCI is to act as the main agency on behalf of the Central Government. Also, for handling foodgrains, it functions as the major instrument of the state policy aimed at achieving the following objectives :

(i) To procure a sizable portion of the marketed surplus of rice at incentive-prices from the farmers on behalf of the Central Government and the State Government.

(ii) To ensure timely release of stocks through the PDS so that the consumer prices do not rise unduly;

(iii) To minimise the inter-seasonal and inter-regional price variations; and,

(iv) To build up sizable buffer stocks of foodgrains.

In order to fulfill these objectives, the FCI undertakes various marketing operations-viz., procurement, storage, movement, distribution, sale and processing of foodgrains and foodstuffs.[18] One of the singular achievements of the government has been of stabilising food prices by ensuring an even spread and undisrupted supply of foodgrains both inter-regionally and inter-temporally. This form of

FIGURE 11

ORGANISATIONAL CHART OF FOOD CORPORATION OF INDIA, REGIONAL OFFICE, JAMMU

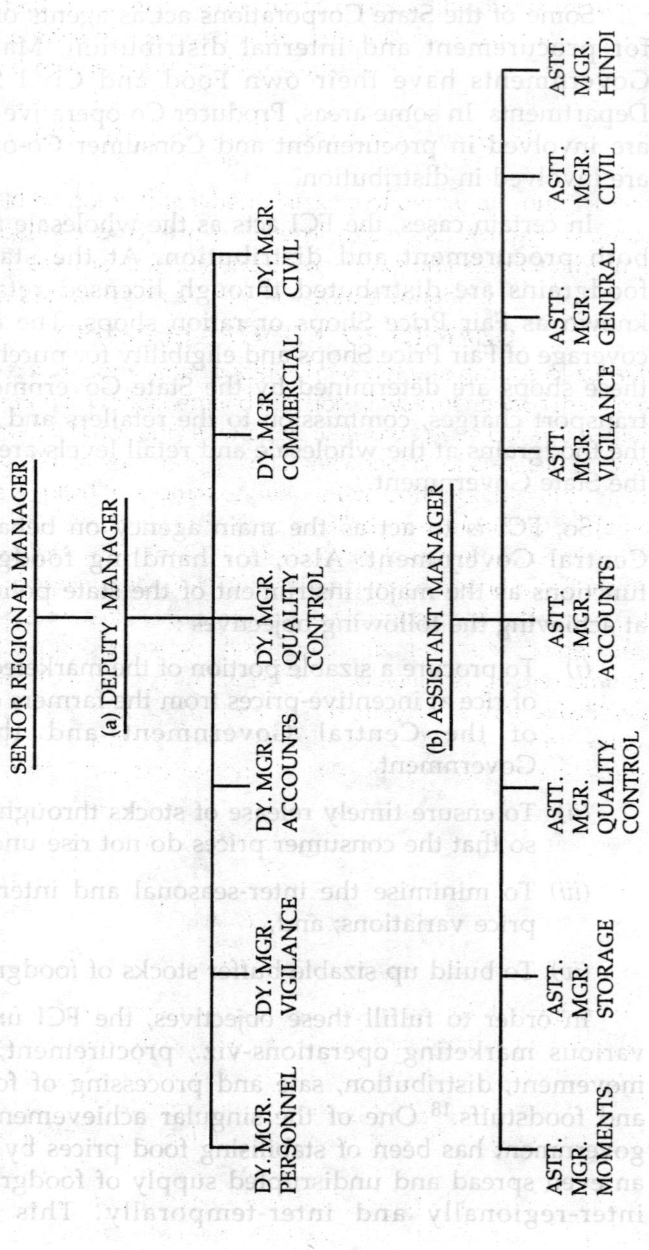

intervention has been an important instrument in combating poverty and hunger.

Though there is a case for reducing the cost of FCI operations by limiting the scope of its wide ranging functions and reducing the volume of its operations, the government has to retain its command over food resources at the regional level. Hence reaching food supplies at subsidised rates to food deficit areas should be a more effective policy in improving living standards than giving purchasing power in the hands of the poor in food deficit area.[19]

Public Distribution System has been introduced in the Jammu Division since long through the Food and Supplies department with the following objectives:

(a) To work as a wholesale dealer to lift rice, wheat & sugar from the procurement agencies.

(b) To ensure regular and prompt supply of essential commodities to the Fair Price Shops; and

(c) To take up distribution of all essential commodities through out the state in a uniform manner especially to the down trodden and economically weak sections who cannot purchase the essential commodities at the open market rates.

Social emphasis is being given on opening of more fair price shops in accordance with the priority given to the scheme of PDS by its inclusion in the 20-point economic programme. In order to provide more facilities in the remote areas, the department utilises the mobile vans to deliver the rationed items to the rationees at their door-steps. There has been increase in the monthly allocation of rice, wheat and sugar from the present 36,000 Mts., 20,000 Mts., and 3,262 Mts., respectively to 44,000 Mts., 30,000 Mts., and 43,000 Mts., in view of the extension of the PDS to the projected population of 1991 in the state.[20]

The State Government has also stressed the need for formulating a regular movement plan so that the supply of foodgrains to the whole state is regulated and buffer-stocking is made well in time in the remote and inaccessible areas. Urgent steps have been taken for creating adequate storage godown facilities all over the state and a clearance of Rs. 450 lakh construction programme which envisages construction of 33 godowns at various remote and far-flung places in the state has been implemented. 20 godowns having capacity of 3,800 Mts. of foodgrains in Leh, Kargil, Doda and Udhampur districts have been constructed with the deptartment's own resources.

In J&K state, the entire Ladakh region, some part of Udhampur District and entire Doda District have been brought under the RPDS. Out of total 12 Blocks which come under Desert development Programme in Ladakh region, five Blocks in Leh district which are namely Nayome, Durbuk, Nubra, Leh and Khalsi while seven blocks of Kargil district namely Kargil, Drass, Shergul, Shaker Chiktan, Sankoora, Teastiry and Zanskar. All the 14 blocks of Doda District and eight blocks of Udhampur District have been brought under DPAP. In addition to above 23 more blocks of Districts Rajouri, Poonch, Kupwara and Baramulla have also been brought under this RPDS scheme.

In Jammu Division 131 additional outlets are to be started, 59 in Doda District and 72 in Udhampur District. The 13 items of essential commodities i.e., kerosene oil, wheat, sugar, rice, atta, tea, soap, controlled cloth, match boxes, pulses, edible oils, iodized salt and exercise note-books have been proposed to be kept in the list of PDS.[21]

In eight blocks of Udhampur District, there has been dismal performance in all the identified blocks as far as implementation of this scheme of RPDS is concerned. The Udhampur District administration has utterly failed to reorient the PDS especially in reaching the remote and hilly specified areas, whereas the Food & Supplies Department continues to claim that items like atta, rice, sugar and kerosene are being distributed through over 200 outlets in Udhampur District.

An important aspect of the PDS is the form of organisational set up of the Food and Supplies Department which influences the performance of the scheme. One Directorate of Food and supplies and three Deputy Directors at the Division level monitor the supplies of foodgrains and other essential commodities in the whole Division. At the Tehsil level, there are Tehsil Supply Officers who look after the functioning of the PDS in their respective Tehsils. Besides, the Assistant Director, Trade and store, Jammu, arranges supplies of foodgrains and sugar for dispatching the same to stores/ sub-stores in the urban and the rural areas of the Division. Also, there is an Assistant Director Mills who looks after the milling of wheat of Roller Flour Mills. The organisational set up of the Food and supplies Deptt. is as follows :

The study reveals that the organisational set up at the central, state and district levels seems to be weak in Jammu region. The operational dimensions of the PDS determine the style of management and its effectiveness in delivering the goods. So, this study is intended to be an assessment of the actual working of PDS in this region especially after launching of revamped PDS (RPDS) which, amongst other things, extend the benefit of specially subsidised central issue price. Apart from this, the RPDS areas are also given additional allocations of rice and wheat with effect from June 1992.

Having observed the general background with regard to availability of foodgrain distribution from PDS and other related factors in the two districts surveyed, it can now be proceeded to look at the study areas and analyse the data obtained from the field survey. The picture that emerges from the analysis of field data in respect of the agencies involved in the functioning of PDS in Jammu Region, is as given below:

First of all, information is collected about the main causes for the origin of this PDS policy in the country and Govt's main objectives in establishing Fair Price Shops. The officials of the FCI and the Food and Supplies Department give maximum responses regarding these causes and objectives of PDS.

FIGURE 12
ORGANISATIONAL CHART OF FOOD & SUPPLIES DEPTT. JAMMU

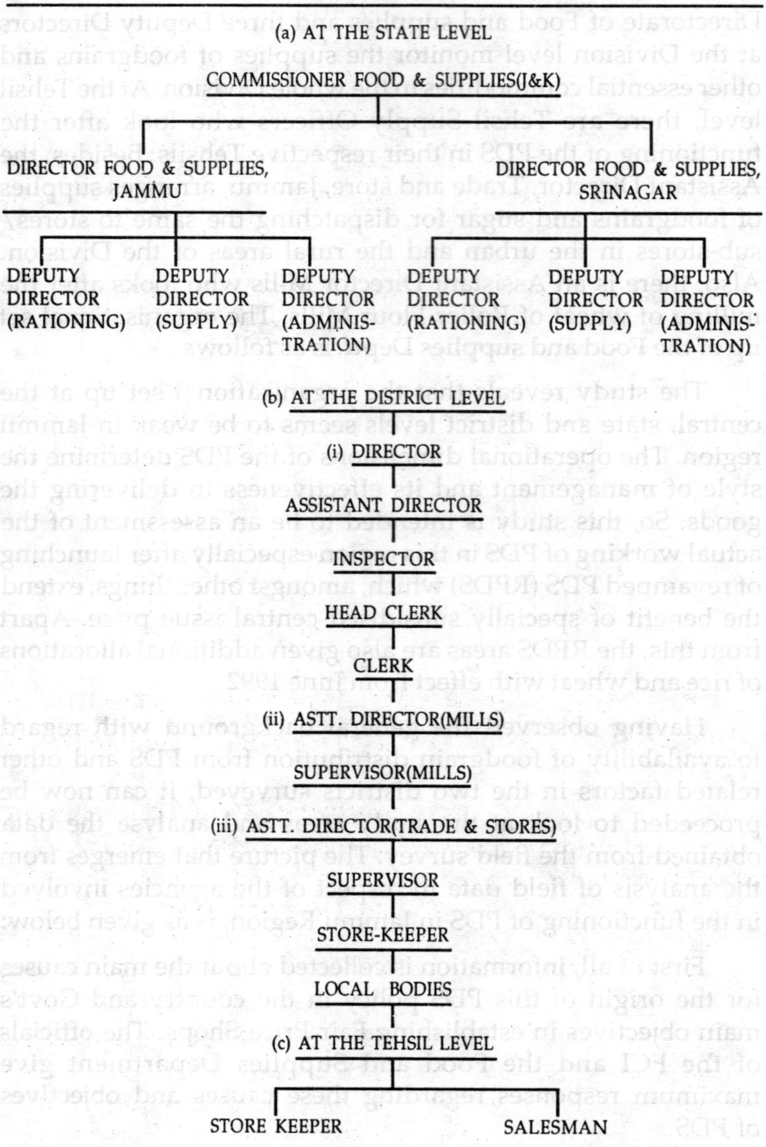

The Table 3.4 shows that in the urban areas, the respondents have given first rank i.e. 33.33 per cent to the first cause drought, famine and war conditions'. The rural respondents have also given the first rank i.e. 40.00 per cent to this cause. The urban respondents have given first and fourth rank i.e. 23.33 per cent to the second cause 'inflation' and the rural respondents have given the same the fourth rank i.e. 30.00 per cent.

The other results of the Table 3.4 depict that there is a very small difference between the responses of both the urban as well as the rural respondents in giving ranks to the other causes like 'market imperfections', 'to generate downward pressure on open market', 'lack of distributive justice' and 'poverty'. No one has given any response about any other cause for the origin of this PDS policy.

Regarding the objectives of the Government in establishing fair price shops, the respondents are of the opinion that the main objective is 'supply of commodities at the reasonable prices' i.e. why, the first rank is given in maximum number i.e. 33.33 per cent and 40.00 per cent by both the urban and the rural respondents.

The other objective 'to serve the poor and the vulnerable sections', has been awarded second rank in maximum number i.e. 23.34 percent by the urban respondents whereas the rural respondents have again given it the first rank in maximum number i.e. 30.00 per cent.

Rest of the results in the table show that both the urban and the rural respondents have not given first three ranks in maximum number to the other main objectives of the government in establishing the Fair Price Shops.

Thus, it is observed during the survey that the perceptions and the views about the origin of this PDS policy and Government's main objectives of both the urban and the rural respondents are quite the same in all aspects.

The respondents have also been asked if the services rendered by the fair price shops are adequate. In response to

Table 3.4

Responses of the Agencies Regarding the main causes for Origin of PDS Policy and Government's Objectives in establishing Fair Price Shops

Part - A Causes

Ranks	Urban No. %age	Rural No. %age	Urban No. %age	Rural No. %age	Urban No. %age	Rural No. %age	Urban No. %age	Rural No. %age	Urban No. %age	Rural No. %age	Urban No. %age	Rural No. %age	Urban No. %age	Rural No. %age
I	10	8	7	3	3	2	4	2	4	3	2	2	0	0
	33.33	40.00	23.33	15.00	10.00	10.00	13.33	10.00	13.33	15.00	6.67	10.00	0.00	0.00
II	8	5	6	4	5	3	4	3	4	3	3	2	0	0
	26.67	25.00	20.00	20.00	16.67	15.00	13.33	15.00	13.33	15.00	10.00	10.00	0.00	0.00
III	5	3	6	5	6	4	5	3	5	3	3	2	0	0
	16.67	15.00	20.00	25.00	20.00	20.00	16.67	15.00	16.67	15.00	10.00	10.00	0.00	0.00
IV	6	2	7	6	5	3	4	4	5	2	3	3	0	0
	20.00	10.00	23.33	30.00	16.67	15.00	13.33	20.00	16.67	10.00	10.00	15.00	0.00	0.00
V	1	2	4	2	6	8	6	3	7	2	6	3	0	0
	3.33	10.00	13.33	10.00	20.00	40.00	20.00	15.00	23.33	10.00	20.00	15.00	0.00	0.00
VI	0	0	0	0	3	0	5	3	2	3	7	6	0	0

Table 3.4 (Contd.)

Ranks	Urban No. %age	Rural No. %age	Urban No. %age	Rural No. %age	Urban No. %age	Rural No. %age	Urban No. %age	Rural No. %age	Urban No. %age	Rural No. %age	Urban No. %age	Rural No. %age	Urban No. %age	Rural No. %age
	0.00	0.00	0.00	0.00	10.00	0.00	16.67	15.00	6.67	15.00	23.33	30.00	0.00	0.00
N.R	0	0	0	0	2	0	2	2	3	4	6	2	30	20
	0.00	0.00	0.00	0.00	6.67	0.00	6.67	10.00	10.00	20.00	20.00	10.00	100.00	100.00
TOTAL	30	20	30	20	30	20	30	20	30	20	30	20	30	20

(i) Drought, famine and war conditions
(ii) Inflation
(iii) Market imperfections
(iv) To generate downward pressure on open market
(v) Lack of distributive justice
(vi) Poverty
(vii) Any other

Source : As per the survey conducted

Part - B Objectives

Ranks	Urban No.	Rural No.	Urban No.	Rural No.	Urban No.	Rural No.	Urban No.	Rural No.	Urban No.	Rural No.	Urban No.	Rural No.	Urban No.	Rural No.
	%age	%age	%age	%age	%age	%age	%age	%age	%age	%age	%age	%age	%age	%age
I	10	8	6	6	3	4	5	2	5	0	1	0	0	0
	33.33	40.00	20.00	30.00	10.00	20.00	16.67	10.00	16.67	0.00	3.33	0.00	0.00	0.00
II	5	3	7	5	6	2	5	2	4	5	3	3	0	0
	16.67	15.00	23.33	25.00	20.00	10.00	16.67	10.00	13.33	25.00	10.00	15.00	0.00	0.00
III	8	5	6	4	5	3	4	3	4	3	3	2	0	0
	26.67	25.00	20.00	20.00	16.67	15.00	13.33	15.00	13.33	15.00	10.00	10.00	0.00	0.00
IV	6	2	4	3	6	8	4	3	6	4	4	0	0	0
	20.00	10.00	13.33	15.00	20.00	40.00	13.33	15.00	20.00	20.00	13.33	0.00	0.00	0.00
V	1	2	7	2	5	3	7	3	4	5	6	5	0	0
	3.33	10.00	23.33	10.00	16.67	15.00	23.33	15.00	13.33	25.00	20.00	25.00	0.00	0.00
VI	0	0	0	0	2	0	3	3	2	3	4	4	0	0
	0.00	0.00	0.00	0.00	6.67	0.00	10.00	15.00	6.67	15.00	13.33	20.00	0.00	0.00

Part B (Contd.)

Ranks	Urban No. %age	Rural No. %age	Urban No. %age	Rural No. %age	Urban No. %age	Rural No. %age	Urban No. %age	Rural No. %age	Urban No. %age	Rural No. %age	Urban No. %age	Rural No. %age	Urban No. %age	Rural No. %age
N.R.	0	0	0	0	3	0	2	4	5	0	9	6	30	20
	0.00	0.00	0.00	0.00	10.00	0.00	6.67	20.00	16.67	0.00	30.00	30.00	100.00	100.00
Total	30	20	30	20	30	20	30	20	30	20	30	20	30	20

(i) Supply of commodities at resonable prices
(ii) To serve poor and vulnerable sections
(iii) Social service
(iv) Prevention of Black Marketing
(v) Proper distribution
(vi) Price stability
(vii) Any other

Source : As per the Survey Conducted.

Table 3.5
Responses of the Agencies Regarding Services Rendered by the Fair Price Shops

Adequacy of Services

Response	*Urban* *No.*	*Urban* *%*	*Rural* *No.*	*Rural* *%*
Yes	18	16.00	10	50.00
No	10	33.33	8	40.00
No Response	2	6.67	2	10.00
Total	30	100.00	20	100.00

If no, the Reasons

Ranks	*Urban No. %age*	*Rural No. %age*	*Urban No. %age*	*Rural No. %age*	*Urban No. %age*	*Rural No. %age*	*Urban No. %age*	*Rural No. %age*	*Urban No. %age*	*Rural No. %age*	*Urban No. %age*	*Rural No. %age*	*Urban No. %age*	*Rural No. %age*
I	3	1	2	2	3	2	2	1	0	1	0	1	10	8
	30.00	12.50	20.00	25.00	30.00	25.00	20.00	12.50	0.00	12.50	0.00	12.50	16.67	16.67
II	2	2	1	2	2	1	2	1	2	1	1	1	10	8
	20.00	25.00	10.00	25.00	20.00	12.50	20.00	12.50	20.00	12.50	10.00	12.50	16.67	16.67
III	2	1	1	1	1	2	1	2	3	2	2	0	10	8
	20.00	12.50	10.00	12.50	10.00	25.00	10.00	25.00	30.00	25.00	20.00	0.00	16.67	16.67

IV	1	2	2	1	1	1	2	2	2	2	2	0	10	8
	10.00	25.00	20.00	12.50	10.00	12.50	20.00	25.00	20.00	25.00	20.00	0.00	16.67	16.67
V	1	1	2	2	2	1	2	1	1	2	2	1	10	8
	10.00	12.50	20.00	25.00	20.00	12.50	20.00	12.50	10.00	25.00	20.00	12.50	16.67	16.67
VI	1	1	1	0	0	0	1	1	2	0	2	3	7	5
	10.00	12.50	10.00	0.00	0.00	0.00	10.00	12.50	20.00	0.00	20.00	37.50	11.67	10.42
N.R	0	0	1	0	1	1	0	0	0	0	1	2	3	3
	0.00	0.00	10.00	0.00	10.00	12.50	0.00	0.00	0.00	0.00	10.00	25.00	5.00	6.25
Total	10	8	10	8	10	8	10	8	10	8	10	8	60	48

Reasons

(i) Irregular Supply
(ii) Excessive Paper Work
(iii) Lack of Card Allotment
(iv) Inadequate Commission
(v) Poor Quality of Goods
(vi) Lack of Supervision

Source : As per the Survey Conducted

Table 3.6

Responses of the Agencies Regarding Awareness about the Production-cum-distribution scheme under the PDS

Aware About the Scheme

Response	*Urban*		*Rural*	
	No.	*%*	*No.*	*%*
Yes	20	66.67	10	50.00
No	8	26.67	6	30.00
No Response	2	6.66	4	20.00
Total	30	100.00	20	100.00

If yes, the main objectives of the Schemes

Ranks	*Urban* No. %Age	*Rural* No. %Age	*Urban* No. %Age	*Rural* No. %Age	*Urban* No. %Age	*Rural* No. %Age	*Urban* No. %Age	*Rural-* No. %Age	*Total* *Urban* No. %Age	*Rural* No. %Age
I	10 50.00	3 30.00	5 25.00	3 30.00	5 25.00	2 20.00	0 0.00	2 20.00	20 25.00	10 25.00
II	6 30.00	2 20.00	6 30.00	1 10.00	5 25.00	3 30.00	3 15.00	4 40.00	20 25.00	10 25.00

III	3	1	2	4	4	2	5	3	14	10
	15.00	10.00	10.00	40.00	20.00	20.00	25.00	30.00	17.50	25.00
IV	1	2	4	1	3	2	6	1	14	6
	5.00	20.00	20.00	10.00	15.00	20.00	30.00	10.00	17.50	15.00
N.R	0	2	3	1	3	1	6	0	12	4
	0.00	20.00	15.00	10.00	15.00	10.00	30.00	0.00	15.00	10.00
Total	20	10	20	10	20	10	20	10	80	40

Objectives

(i) Adequacy of the Rural Coverage

(ii) Procurement by Public Agencies

(iii) Extension of Commodity Coverage

(iv) Encouragement of Public Participation

Source : As per the Survey Conducted

Table 3.7

Responses of the Agencies Regarding following the same norms and conditions in urban & rural areas

Follow the same norms and conditions

Response	*Urban*		*Rural*	
	No.	%	*No.*	%
Yes	18	16.00	8	40.00
No	10	33.33	8	40.00
No Response	2	6.67	4	20.00
Total	30	100.00	20	100.00

If No, the Differences

Ranks	*Urban No. %age*	*Rural No. %age*	*Urban No. %age*	*Rural No. %age*	*Urban No. %age*	*Rural No. %age*	*Urban No. %age*	*Rural No. %age*	*Urban No. %age*	*Rural No. %age*	*Urban No. %age*	*Rural No. %age*	*Total Urban No. %age*	*Total Rural No. %age*
I	3	1	2	0	3	2	2	1	1	1	0	1	10	8
	20.00	12.50	20.00	25.00	30.00	25.00	20.00	12.50	10.00	12.580	0.00	12.50	16.67	16.67
II	3	2	1	2	2	1	2	1	1	1	1	1	10	8
	30.00	25.00	10.00	25.00	20.00	12.50	20.00	12.50	10.00	12.50	10.00	12.50	16.67	16.67
III	2	1	1	1	1	2	1	2	3	2	2	0	10	8
	20.00	12.50	10.00	12.50	10.00	25.00	10.00	25.00	30.00	25.00	20.00	0.00	16.67	16.67

IV	1	2	2	1	1	1	2	2	2	2	2	0	10	8
	10.00	25.00	20.00	12.50	10.00	12.50	20.00	25.00	20.00	25.00	20.00	0.00	16.67	16.67
V	1	1	2	2	2	1	2	1	1	2	2	1	10	8
	10.00	12.50	20.00	25.00	20.00	12.50	20.00	12.50	10.00	25.00	20.00	12.50	16.67	16.67
VI	1	1	1	0	0	0	1	1	2	0	2	3	7	5
	10.00	12.50	10.00	0.00	0.00	0.00	10.00	12.50	20.00	0.00	20.00	37.50	11.67	10.42
N.R.	0	0	1	0	1	1	0	0	0	0	1	2	3	3
	0.00	0.00	10.00	0.00	10.00	12.50	0.00	0.00	0.00	0.00	10.00	25.00	5.00	6.25
Total	10	8	10	8	10	8	10	8	10	8	10	8	60	48

Differences

(i) Transport problems
(ii) Promotional devices
(iii) Corruption and malpractices
(iv) Aware about consumer laws
(v) Complaints are easily redressed
(vi) Control and Supervision over FPSs

Source : As per the Survey Conducted

Table 3.8

Responses of the Agencies Regarding Awareness about the Policies of Revemped PDS Aware about RPDS

Response	*Urban*		*Rural*	
	No.	*%*	*No.*	*%*
Yes	15	50.00	8	40.00
No	12	40.00	8	40.00
No Response	3	10.00	4	20.00
Total	30	100.00	20	100.00

If Yes, the Provisions made

													TOTAL	
Ranks	*Urban No. %age*	*Rural No. %age*	*Urban No. %age*	*Rural No. %age*	*Urban No. %age*	*Rural No. %age*	*Urban No. %age*	*Rural No. %age*	*Urban No. %age*	*Rural No. %age*	*Urban No. %age*	*Rural No. %age*	*Urban No. %age*	*Rural No. %age*
I	3	2	2	2	4	1	3	1	2	1	1	1	15	8
	20.00	25.00	13.33	25.00	26.67	12.50	20.00	12.50	13.33	12.50	6.67	12.50	16.67	16.67
II	3	0	3	1	5	1	3	1	1	2	0	3	15	8
	20.00	0.00	20.00	12.50	33.33	12.50	20.00	12.50	6.67	25.00	0.00	37.50	16.67	16.67
III	2	1	1	1	2	2	2	3	4	1	4	0	15	8
	13.33	12.50	6.67	12.50	13.33	25.00	13.33	37.50	26.67	12.50	26.67	0.00	16.67	16.67

IV	2	2	2	1	1	2	2	2	3	0	5	1	15	8
	13.33	25.00	13.33	12.50	6.67	25.00	13.33	25.00	20.00	0.00	33.33	12.50	16.67	16.67
V	3	1	3	2	1	1	1	1	2	1	3	1	13	7
	20.00	12.50	20.00	25.00	6.67	12.50	6.67	12.50	13.33	12.50	20.00	12.50	14.44	14.58
VI	1	2	2	1	1	1	2	0	2	2	1	2	9	8
	6.67	25.00	13.33	12.50	6.67	12.50	13.33	0.00	13.33	25.00	6.67	25.00	10.00	16.67
N.R	1	0	2	0	1	0	2	0	1	1	1	0	8	1
	6.67	0.00	13.33	0.00	6.67	0.00	13.33	0.00	6.67	12.50	6.67	0.00	8.89	2.08
Total	15	8	15	8	15	8	15	8	15	8	15	8	90	48

PROVISIONS MADE

(i) Reducing the CIP

(ii) Issuing of New Ration Cards

(iii) Forming Vigilance Committiees

(iv) Identifying the Blocks

(v) Getting rid of urban bias

(vi) Opening More Centres

Source : As per the survey conducted

Table 3.9

Responses of the agencies Regarding Awareness about the Objectives and Working of FCI

Aware about the Objectives of FCI

Response	*Urban* No.	*Urban* %	*Rural* No.	*Rural* %
Yes	18	60.00	12	60.00
No	10	33.33	6	30.00
No Response	2	6.67	2	10.00
Total	**30**	**100.00**	**20**	**100.00**

If Yes, the main Objectives of FCI

Ranks	*Urban No. %age*	*Rural No. %age*	*Urban No. %age*	*Rural No. %age*	*Urban No. %age*	*Rural No. %age*	*Urban No. %age*	*Rural- No. %age*	*Total* *Urban No. %age*	*Total* *Rural No. %age*
I	5	5	6	3	4	2	3	2	18	12
	27.78	41.67	33.33	25.00	22.22	16.67	16.67	16.67	25.00	25.00
II	4	3	5	3	5	4	4	2	18	12
	22.22	25.00	27.78	25.00	27.78	33.33	22.22	16.67	25.00	25.00

III	3	2	4	4	4	3	7	3	18	12
	16.67	16.67	22.22	33.33	22.22	25.00	38.89	25.00	25.00	25.00
IV	3	2	2	1	3	2	4	3	12	8
	16.67	16.67	11.11	8.33	16.67	16.67	22.22	25.00	16.67	16.67
N.R	3	0	1	1	2	1	0	2	6	4
	16.67	0.00	5.56	8.33	11.11	8.33	0.00	16.67	8.33	8.33
Total	**18**	**12**	**18**	**12**	**18**	**12**	**18**	**12**	**72**	**48**

Objectives

(i) To build up buffer stocks

(ii) To increase emphasis on strong network

(iii) To increase administrative control

(iv) To minimise inter-seasonal price

Source: As per the survey conducted

the question, the majority of the respondents have indicated that the services are adequate and those who give negative responses are of the opinion that the services are inadequate due to various reasons. Table 3.5 depicts that there is a slight difference between the responses of the respondents regarding the reasons like irregular supply, excessive paper work, lack of proper card allotment, inadequate commission, poor quality of goods and lack of supervision.

Responses have been generated with regard to awareness about the production-cum-distribution scheme under the PDS. Majority of the respondents from both the areas, give positive responses due to some reasons, which they think, are the main objectives of the scheme. First rank is given by 50 per cent of the respondents to the 'Adequacy of rural coverage' objective in the urban areas and 30 per cent have given it first rank in the rural areas. 'Encouragement of public participation' has gained third and fourth ranks in maximum number in the urban areas whereas, in the rural areas, rural perception is not the same. The other results are shown in the Table 3.6.

In response to the question of following the same norms and conditions in the urban and the rural areas, the respondents give 33.33 per cent and 40 per cent responses in the negative, respectively. The main reason for not following the same norms and conditions is the transport problem. Specifically in the remote and hilly areas where the ration commodities are not available in time, corruption and malpractices is another reason for not following the same norms. The other reasons are shown in Table 3.7.

Concerning the same Table as above the question is also asked whether the respondents are aware about the policies of the revamped PDS in the State. Majority of them are of the opinion that they have made some provisions to implement this policy of RPDS in the hilly and remote areas. The policies of RPDS include reducing the CIP, issuing of new ration cards following vigilance committees at the block levels and identifying more blocks to be covered under the RPDS and getting rid of urban-bias. Table 3.8 depicts that there is common perception of RPDS among the respondents of both the urban and the rural areas.

In order to find the reaction of the officials of the FCI regarding the awareness about the objectives and working of FCI, the maximum responses are generated in the positive from both the urban and the rural areas. According to them, the main objective of the FCI is to build up buffer stocks to run this system effectively and the same has been given first rank. The percentage of responses generated is 27.78 per cent in the urban areas and 41.66 per cent in the rural areas. Majority of the urban respondents i.e. 38.89 per cent have given third rank to the objective 'to minimise inter seasonal price variations' whereas the rural respondents have shown a slight difference in giving ranks to this objective. The other responses regarding-some other objectives of the FCI are shown in Table 3.9.

The analysis indicates that the organisational and the managerial structure from the central level down to the district level is weak and lacks unity of purpose. The overall perception of the PDS of both the urban and the rural respondents is not the same. There is a slight difference between the responses of the respondents of both the areas.

REFERENCES

1. Mathur, B.C., : 'Management in Government', 1981, p. 13.
2. Kabra, K.N., & Anil C.I., : 'The PDS in India', 1992, p. 61.
3. Ojha, G.D., 'Organisation & Management of PDS', 1987, p. 53. ls2
4. Kabra, K.N., & Anil C.I., 'The PDS in India', 1992, p. 62.
5. Bapna, S.L., 'Increasing Access to Food—The Indian Experiment' 1980, p. 119.
6. Nawani, N.P., 'Towards Food for All—Ideas for a New PDS', 1995, p. 113.
7. Venugopal, K.R., 'Deliverance from Hunger—The PDS in India', 1992, p. 130.

8. Shenoi, G.V., 'Management of PDS'—The Indian Journal of Public Administration, Vol-XXXVI, Jan-Mar 1990, p. 87.
9. Nawani, N.P., 'Towards Food for All—Ideas for a New PDS', 1995, p. 123.
10. The Economic Times, New Delhi, Feb. 20, 1995, p. 1.
11. The Hindu, Jun. 15, 1995, p. 6..
12. Ojha. Ghanshyam Das., 'Organisation & Management of PDS', 1987, p. 72.
13. Economic Times, New Delhi, Aug. 16, 1994, p. 8.
14. Dev, S. Mahendra, 'The Vulnerable Section and the PDS', Economic & Political Weekly, Aug, 1993, p. 43.
15. Nawani, N.P, 'Towards Food for All—Ideas for a New PDS' 1995, p. 130.
16. Economic Times, New Delhi, Aug. 16, 1994, p. 8.
17. Daily Excelsior, Sep. 24, 1993, p. 3.
18. Ojha, Ghanshyam Das., 'Organisation & Management of PDS' 1987, p. 32.
19. The Economic Times, New Delhi, Sep. 9, 1993, p. 6.
20. As per the Records of Food and Supplies Deptt, Jammu.
21. As per the Information recieved by the Official Records of Directorate of Food & Supplies, Jammu.

Chapter-4

Operational Aspects of Fair Price Shops

Access to the PDS facilities depends on a variety of factors, among which organisation, performance and viability of Fair Price Shops (the retail supply outlets) are of crucial significance. Apart from some very important general factors affecting FPS operations, the augmentation of supplies through the states' own procurement and the extent of coverage, there are some specific factors that need to be analysed. This set of factors is related to the administrative arrangements made for public distribution and which directly affect the operations and viability of licensed retail outlets. Some of the important variables that directly reflect the administrative arrangements are the number of cards or ration units attached to each retail outlet, number of FPSs and their size, their location, various aspects of choice of FPS licencee, arrangements for supplying stocks of PDS commodities to FPS, profit margins allowed to FPS dealer, control and regulation of FPS by Civil Supplies Authorities, rationed and non-rationed commodities sold, age-profile of FPS, location of wholesale stocking Depots, transport cost of FPS, frequency of inspection, general complaints by FPS dealer and some other miscellaneous factors.

To ascertain the first hand information about the operational aspects of the FPSs and to assess their performance, a detailed sample survey has been conducted covering 200 retail outlets in both the urban and the rural areas of Jammu

Region. The information obtained through the questionnaire from the FPS dealers is analysed and the inferences that have been drawn on various issues are given below :

(i) Ration Cards/Units Attached to each FPS:

The administrative decision regarding the number of cards or ration units to be served by each shop has a vital bearing on two major objectives of public distribution. On the one hand, the number of cards attached determines the potential turn over that can be achieved in each shop thereby leading to its financial viability. On the other hand, the card/unit population also determines the degree of consumer access available to those attached to each shop and in turn, leading to the proper and adequate utilisation of public distribution facilities by the consumers.

A large number of cards or units attached to a shop may improve the potential viability of the outlet but at the cost of consumer access, unless adequately efficient retailing within the stipulated issue period and the regularity and adequacy of sales and stocking are also achieved simultaneously. Therefore, while deciding on the population to be served by any particular outlet, careful consideration is required for attaining the right balance between these two objectives.

It is observed during the survey that as far as the number of cards to be served is concerned, 31.50 per cent of the private fair price shops do not specify the number of ration cards allotted to them. According to the private fair price shop dealers, no private fair price shop is given the specified number of cards. All these shops are allotted uniform monthly quotas irrespective of the number of consumers to be served. These quotas, as expressed by the dealers, are subject to abrupt changes made from time to time without giving any prior notice. Since there is no specification of consumers over the quotas, they issue ration on all the cards produced by the people of neighbouring areas till the stocks get exhausted. This type of non-specification of cards and quotas, results in unplanned management of shops and consumer dissatisfaction. This also results in strained relations between the dealers and the consumers as they abuse each

Figure - 13

Responses Regarding Total Cards Served

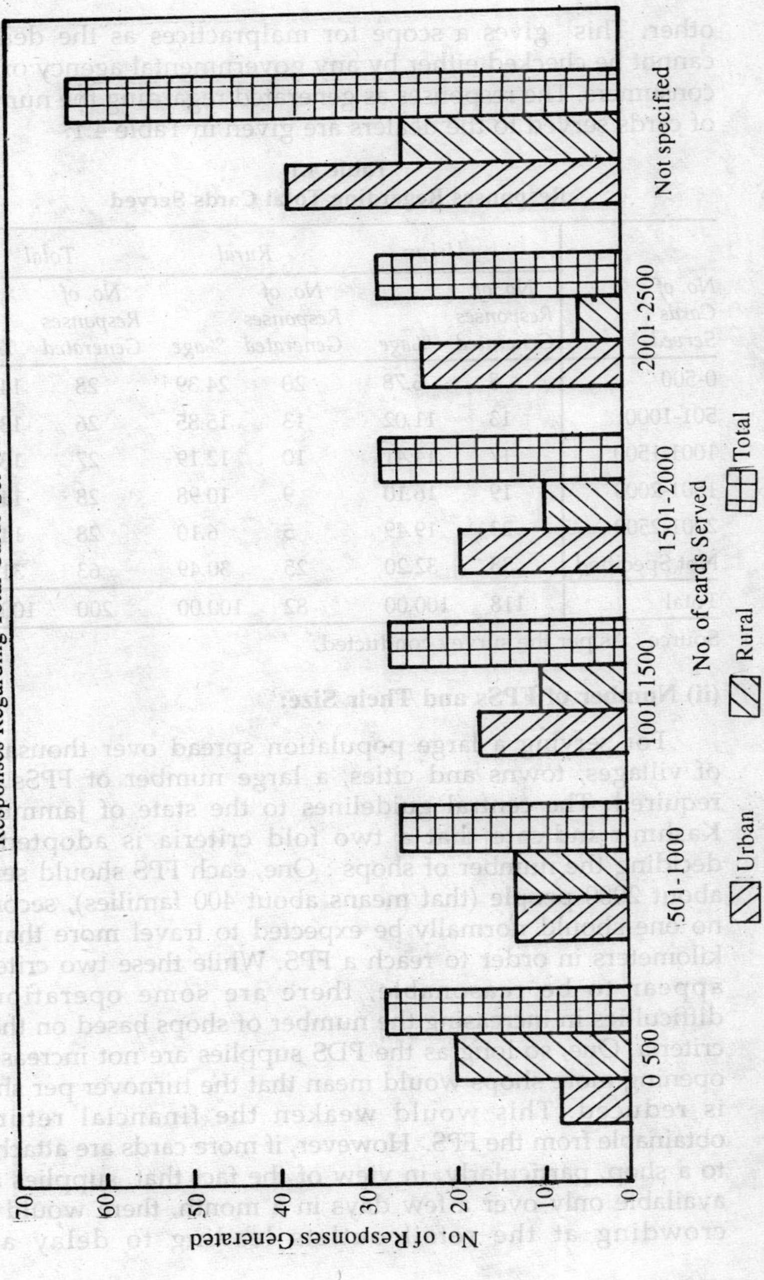

other. This gives a scope for malpractices as the dealers cannot be checked either by any governmental agency or the consumers. The responses as generated regarding the number of cards served to the dealers are given in Table 4.1.

Table 4.1
Responses Regarding Total Cards Served

No. of Cards Served	*Urban*		*Rural*		*Total*	
	No. of Responses Generated	*%age*	*No. of Responses Generated*	*%age*	*No. of Responses Generated*	*%age*
0-500	8	6.78	20	24.39	28	14.00
501-1000	13	11.02	13	15.85	26	13.00
1001-1500	17	14.41	10	12.19	27	13.50
1501-2000	19	16.10	9	10.98	28	14.00
2001-2500	23	19.49	5	6.10	28	14.00
Not Specified	38	32.20	25	30.49	63	31.50
Total	118	100.00	82	100.00	200	100.00

Source : As per the survey conducted.

(ii) Number of FPSs and Their Size:

For serving a large population spread over thousands of villages, towns and cities, a large number of FPSs are required. The central guidelines to the state of Jammu & Kashmir indicate that a two fold criteria is adopted in deciding the number of shops : One, each FPS should serve about 2000 people (that means about 400 families), second, no one should normally be expected to travel more than 5 kilometers in order to reach a FPS. While these two criteria appear to be reasonable, there are some operational difficulties in increasing the number of shops based on these criteria. One, so long as the PDS supplies are not increased, opening more shops would mean that the turnover per shop is reduced. This would weaken the financial returns obtainable from the FPS. However, if more cards are attached to a shop, particularly, in view of the fact that, supplies are available only over a few days in a month, there would be crowding at the retail outlets leading to delay and inconvenience to the consumers. Such difficulties become all the more acute in the rural areas.

Given an efficient functioning and meaningful PDS, the needs of the villagers may be met without necessarily going in for the adoption of the principle of one village, one shop. In any case, by opening shops in the weekly haats in the rural areas, the net work of PDS retail outlets can be made more effective. In areas with very poor transport facilities and dispersed villages, mobile shops, not necessarily on motorised vehicles, can be used for the purpose.

(iii) Choice of FPS Dealer:

The PDS amounts to a limited introduction of state trading in essential commodities. One of the important administrative arrangements required for the PDS is that of licensing an agency for acting as a retail outlet. The Food and Supplies Deptt., generally, acts as a wholesale distribution agency to the FPS though this also runs a few retail outlets in Jammu Region. In the valley region of Jammu & Kashmir, the retail outlets are departmental shops owned and managed by the civil Supplies Department but in Jammu Region, both private individuals and co-operatives have also been authorised to run the FPSs. Thus, a two-tier system is prevalent in Jammu & Kashmir.

In the Jammu Region, both in the urban and the rural areas, the largest single group of FPSs are run by private individuals who are authorised by the State Civil Supplies Department to supply the PDS commodities at the fixed prices to the card holders according to the fixed entitlements. Such authorisations are given on the basis of inviting applications and the State Government has specifically laid down criteria on the basis of which district authorities choose the PDS licencee. Preference is generally given, next only to co-operatives, of people belonging to scheduled castes and scheduled tribes, unemployed persons, ex-servicemen and the educated un-employed. From some of the preferred categories, either no application fee is charged or lower security deposits are insisted upon. However, the rates of profit margins allowed to the licencees are the same. Among the terms and conditions of dealership, there is a clear stipulation that either no goods other than the PDS can be sold by the fair price shop dealer or if the dealer was to sell commodities other than the PDS, he would not deal in the same commodities as are covered under the PDS purview.

Majority of the shops are found to be privately owned and only a few shops are managed by the co-operatives and the government controlled agencies. The ownership pattern, thus, shows a dominance of privately owned shops. The general consensus is that even though it would have been better to allow an educated unemployed to earn his living by running a FPS, the business is not really of a scale which can afford such people, a living on a regular basis especially when the profit margins allowed are quite low. Infact, the prevailing impression is that the FPS dealers, because of these low margins of income from the PDS business have to bank upon some other sources of income to sustain themselves.

The main objectives of the FPS dealers in running this business, as revealed during the survey, are 'profit', followed by 'previous business', 'occupation of the dealer', 'monthly income' and 'customer satisfaction'. In the urban areas, 29.82 per cent respondents have given first rank, 26.32 per cent have given third rank and the remaining have given other lower ranks to 'profit' as the main objective. In the rural areas, 26.83 per cent have given it third rank.

'Previous business' is the second important objective to run this business. In the urban areas, 17.54 per cent respondents have given first and fourth ranks to this objective followed by 38.60 per cent who have given third rank and the remaining have given other lower ranks. 3.52 per cent respondents have not given any response for this objective. In the rural areas, 31.71 per cent respondents have given first rank to this objective followed by 26.83 per cent who have given third rank with the remaining having given other lower ranks to this aforesaid objective.

'Occupation of the shop owner', 'monthly income' and 'customer satisfaction' are also viewed as the main objectives of the FPS dealers. 49.12 per cent respondents in the urban areas and 58.54 per cent respondents in the rural areas have not given any response to the objective 'customer satisfaction'. It shows that a very few dealers deal in this business with this main objective as exhibited in Table 4.2.

(iv) Arrangements for Supplying Stocks of PDS Commodities to the FPSs :

A number of rules and regulations are imposed on the FPS dealers as part of terms and conditions under which they are authorised to distribute the PDS commodities. These cover such matters as business hours, the procedure for issue of receipts to the card holders and the maintenance of books of accounts. The periodicity of the sales, the method of arranging supplies from the wholesale depot to the FPS, the distance, the frequency, the transport charges for making delivery of stocks to the FPS, the quality of the goods supplied and the methods of making payments for the stocks given to the FPS are other important factors which affect the cost of the FPS operations.

It has been observed during the survey that the majority of the shop owners, in the rural areas, are of the view that they require half a day for obtaining orders for the issue of foodgrains and another half for receiving the commodities and on an average, a day for transporting the supplies to their shops. In this way, two to three days are spent on obtaining orders, receiving grains, transporting them and then, distributing the same to the people.

(v) Profit Margins Allowed to FPS Dealers :

The main objective of FPS dealer in obtaining a licence is the desire to earn the profit margins confirred by the Government on regular and assured sales. The profit margin given to the FPS dealer is added to the ex-godown price in order to arrive at the issue price. Thus, the profit margin allowed to the dealer is borne by the consumers. For different commodities, different rates of margins are allowed. In addition to the margin, the FPS dealer is allowed to retain

Table 4.2
Responses Regarding main Objectives of the Fair Price Shop Dealers

Objectives

Ranks	Urban No. %age	Rural No. %age	Urban No. %age	Rural No. %age	Urban No. %age	Rural No. %age	Urban No. %age	Rural No. %age	Urban No. %age	Rural No. %age	Urban No. %age	Rural No. %age	Total Urban No. %age	Total Rural No. %age
I	34	18	20	26	32	20	14	12	14	4	0	2	114	82
	29.82	21.95	17.54	31.71	28.07	24.39	12.28	14.63	12.28	4.88	0.00	2.44	16.67	16.67
II	8	8	16	20	34	16	32	22	14	12	10	4	114	82
	7.02	9.76	14.04	24.39	29.82	19.51	28.07	26.83	12.28	14.63	8.77	4.88	16.67	16.67
III	30	22	44	22	14	14	8	8	2	4	0	0	98	70
	26.32	26.83	38.60	26.83	12.28	17.07	7.02	9.76	1.75	4.88	0.00	0.00	14.33	14.23
IV	18	8	20	10	22	20	18	16	2	2	0	0	80	56
	15.79	9.76	17.54	12.20	19.30	24.39	15.79	19.51	1.75	2.44	0.00	0.00	11.70	11.38
V	4	4	8	2	6	2	12	6	24	12	0	4	54	30
	3.51	4.88	7.02	2.44	5.26	2.44	10.53	7.32	21.05	14.63	0.00	4.88	7.89	6.10
VI	2	4	2	0	0	2	0	0	2	0	4	6	10	10
	1.75	4.88	1.75	0.00	0.00	2.44	0.00	0.00	1.75	0.00	3.51	7.32	1.46	2.03

N.R	18 15.79	18 21.95	4 3.51	2 2.44	6 5.26	8 9.76	30 26.32	18 21.95	56 49.12	48 58.54	100 87.72	66 80.49	214 31.29	162 32.93
Total	114	82	114	82	114	82	114	82	114	82	114	82	684	492

Objectives

(i) Profit

(ii) Previous Business

(iii) Occupation of Dealers

(iv) Monthly Income

(v) Customer satsifaction

(vi) Any other

Source: As per the survey conducted

Note :

Total no. of of respondents	118
No response	4
Total No. of responses generated	114

the gunny bag free of cost Table 4.3 shows the responses of the dealers with respect to the satisfaction with the monthly salary or the commission on the sales. Infact, the profit margins are essentially a commission or a remuneration given to the FPS dealers for discharging the function of distribution of PDS commodities in the specified quantities at the fixed prices over specified intervals of time to specified group of people. There is hardly any significant element of risk involved in PDS operations, except for the fluctuating level of the off-take by the consumers. However, the level of off-take by the consumers depends partly on the FPS dealers' behaviour, decisions and efficiency.

Table 4.3

Responses regarding satisfaction with Monthly Salary/CO

Response	*Urban*		*Rural*	
	No.	*%*	*No.*	*%*
Yes	58	49.15	36	43.90
No	58	49.15	46	56.10
No Response	2	1.70	0	0.00
Total	118	100.00	82	100.00

If no, the Reasons Regarding Dissatisfaction

Ranks	*Urban No. %age*	*Rural No. %age*	*Urban No. %age*	*Rural No. %age*	*Urban No. %age*	*Rural No. %age*	*Total Urban No. % age*	*Total Rural No. % age*
I	28 48.28	20 43.48	18 31.03	12 26.09	12 20.69	14 30.43	58 33.33	46 33.33
II	16 27.59	10 21.74	22 37.93	20 43.48	18 31.03	14 30.43	56 32.18	44 31.88
III	12 20.69	12 26.09	16 27.59	14 30.43	12 20.69	14 30.43	40 22.99	40 28.99
N.R	2 3.45	4 8.70	2 3.45	0 0.00	16 27.59	4 8.70	20 11.49	8 5.80
Total	58	46	58	46	58	46	174	138

Reasons of Dissatisfaction
(i) Traditional Line, (iii) Absence if alternative
(ii) In anticipation of better service

Source : As per the survey conducted

(vi) Behaviour of the Customers :

An attempt has been made to know the opinion of the dealers about the behaviour of the customers at the time of drawing their ration from the PDS shops. 42.37 per cent of the urban respondents and 39.02 per cent of the rural respondents have said that the behaviour of the customers is quite pleasant towards them whereas 30.51 per cent of the urban respondents and 31.71 per cent of the rural respondents are of the view that the customers get irritated at forming long queues which according to them, are time consuming and upset their other engagements. Uncertainties about the arrival of stocks and sudden arrival of stocks also make them irritated. Responses, regarding indifferent behaviour of the customers towards the dealers, are also exhibited in Table 4.4.

Table 4.4
Responses Regarding Rating the Behaviour of Customers

Responses	*Urban*		*Rural*		*Total*	
	No. of Resp.	*%age*	*No. of Resp.*	*%age*	*No. of Resp.*	*%age*
Pleasent	50	42.37	32	39.02	82	41.00
Irritating	36	30.51	26	31.71	62	31.00
Indifferent	32	27.12	24	29.27	56	28.00
Total	118	100.00	82	100.00	200	100.00

Source : As per the survey conducted

Inspite of the customers' behaviour towards the dealers, responses have also been generated regarding their experiences while dealing with the customers at the fair price shops. As Table 4.5 exhibits, 41.82 per cent of the urban respondents and 38.46 per cent of the rural respondents have given first rank to the experience 'irritating customers abuse the dealers'. 'Lumpen elements threaten the dealers' is another main experience narrated by the dealers. In the urban areas, 34.54 per cent respondents

Table 4.5
Responses Regarding Experiences While Dealing with Customers

	Experiences								Total	
Ranks	*Urban* *No.* *%age*	*Rural* *No.* *%age*	*Urban* *No.* *%age*	*Rural* *No.* *%age*	*Urban* *No.* *%age*	*Rural* *No.* *%age*	*Urban* *No.* *%age*	*Rural* *No.* *%age*	*Urban* *No.* *%age*	*Rural* *No.* *%age*
I	46	30	16	30	34	12	14	6	110	78
	41.82	38.46	14.55	38.46	30.91	15.38	12.73	7.69	25.00	25.00
II	16	18	34	28	24	20	36	12	110	78
	14.55	23.08	30.91	35.90	21.82	25.64	32.73	15.38	25.00	25.00
III	18	12	38	14	32	38	6	6	94	70
	16.36	15.38	34.55	17.95	29.09	48.72	5.45	7.69	21.36	22.44
IV	18	10	10	4	16	6	24	16	68	36
	16.36	12.82	9.09	5.13	14.55	7.69	21.82	20.51	15.45	11.54
N.R	12	8	12	2	4	2	30	38	58	50
	10.91	10.26	10.91	2.56	3.64	2.56	27.27	48.72	13.18	16.03
TOTAL	110	78	110	78	110	78	110	78	440	312

Experiences	Urban	Rural
(i) Irregular Customers abouse the Dealer		
(ii) Lumpen Elements Threaten		
(iii) Manhandling & Gheroing		
(iv) Pressure from influential people		
No. of Total Responses	118	82
No Response	8	4
No. of Responses Gener	110	78

Source : As per the survey conducted

have given third rank followed by 30.91 per cent who have given second rank and further followed by 14.55 per cent who have given first rank to this experience. In the rural areas, 38.46 per cent of the respondents have given first rank to the same experience. 35.90 per cent of the respondents have also given it the second rank. Other experiences like 'manhandling and gheraoing of the dealers' and 'pressure from the influential persons' are also experienced by the dealers. It is interesting to note that 48.72 per cent respondents in the rural areas and 27.27 per cent respondents in the urban areas, have not responded to the experience, 'pressure from the influential persons'.

(vii) Services Rendered by Fair Price Shops :

38.98 per cent of the urban dealers and 56.10 per cent of the rural dealers are of the opinion that they provide adequate services to their customers. A very few number of the dealers of both the areas, provide the services to some extent as shown in Table 4.6. Thus, the inferences show that this difference in the responses could be traced to the quota allotted to a shop and the number of cards served by the FPSs.

Table 4.6
Response Regarding Providing adequate Services to Customers

Responses	*Urban*		*Rural*		*Total*	
	No. of Resp.	*%age*	*No. of Resp.*	*%age*	*No. of Resp.*	*%age*
Yes	46	38.98	46	56.10	92	46.00
No	38	32.20	22	26.83	60	30.00
To Some Extent	34	28.82	14	17.07	48	24.00
Total	118	100.00	82	100.00	200	100.00

Source : As per the survey conducted

Responses have also been generated with respect to the prevention of providing better services to the customers, as exhibited in Table 4.7. Majority of the dealers have given responses regarding various causes viz. inadequate commission, non-availability of stocks in time from the government itself, etc., Which create hurdles in providing better services to their customers. Some dealers are of the view that corruption at the level of supervisory staff compels them to indulge in black marketing and other malpractices. It is also observed during the survey that the dealers are conscious of consumer dissatisfaction and their own ineffectiveness to deal with it.

(viii) Rationed and Non-Rationed Commodities Sold:

As a general rule, a retail outlet is not allowed to sell non-rationed commodities from the same shop floor. However, in some cases, the sale of non-rationed commodities is allowed in order to provide a certain level of viability in retail activities. The non-rationed commodities allowed to be sold are most often other than the commodities supplied under the PDS. This disallowance of such sales, is with the intention of avoiding adulteration of commodities like rice and sugar, which are available in various grades of quality in the open market and also to make sure that PDS consumers are not neglected at the cost of the general consumers. Moreover, the simultaneous sale of rationed and non-rationed commodities from the same shop floor is avoided in order to reduce the possible typing up of sales of slow moving non-rationed items with rationed items like sugar, etc.

It has been observed during the survey that in both the urban and the rural areas of Jammu Region, the sale of rationed and non-rationed commodities from the same retail point is allowed in order to improve the viability of FPS.

Table 4.7
Responses regarding prevention in providing better services to Customers

Ranks	Urban No. %age	Rural No. %age	Urban No. %age	Rural No. %age	Urban No. %age	Rural No. %age	Total Urban No. %age	Total Rural No. %age
I	44	24	50	40	12	14	106	78
	41.51	30.77	47.17	51.28	11.32	17.95	33.33	33.33
II	24	24	30	22	46	28	100	74
	22.64	30.77	28.30	28.21	43.40	35.90	31.45	31.62
III	32	28	16	14	34	28	82	70
	30.19	35.90	15.09	17.95	32.08	35.90	25.79	29.91
N.R	6	2	10	2	14	8	30	12
	5.66	2.56	9.43	2.56	13.21	10.26	9.43	5.13
Total	106	78	106	78	106	78	318	234

Reasons

(i) Inadequate Commission

(ii) Non-availability of Stock

(iii) Excessive paper work

N.R = U = 180 – 12=106, R = 82 – 4=78

Source : As per the survey conducted

Very few FPS dealers are of the opinion that while selling non-rationed commodities, they are not getting any benefit from the same.

The survey has revealed that majority of the people of Jammu Region purchase and consume the ration items supplied under the PDS. Responses have also been generated with regard to the consumers of different income groups from the dealers' point of view. In the urban areas, 44.07 per cent respondents have given first rank to the income Group-I (Income < 2,000 p.m) followed by 22.03 per cent who have given it the second rank. In the rural areas, 41.46 per cent respondents have also given first rank to this income group followed by 26.83 per cent who have given it the second rank. Other lower ranks are also given to this income group. It is interesting to note that the respondents of both the areas have given fourth rank and second rank respectively i.e. 32.20 per cent and 31.70 per cent to the Income Group above Rs. 6,000) as exhibited in Table 4.8.

It indicates that all the people of all the income groups prefer to purchase the ration items from the FPSs Table 4.9 shows the responses generated with respect to the purchase of the ration items for various reasons. In the urban areas, 54.24 per cent respondents have given first rank to 'lower price' as the main reason and 18.65 per cent have given second rank. 5.08 have not given any response. Similarly, in the rural areas, 56.10 per cent respondents have given it first rank and 21.95 per cent have also given second rank to this reason. Equally important reason for the preference to purchase the PDS items is 'easy availability'. In the urban areas, 52.54 per cent respondents have given it the second rank whereas, in the rural areas, 39.02 per cent have given first rank to the same reason. The respondents of both the areas have given third rank to another reason 'good quality'.

Table 4.8
Response regarding consumers cconsuming ration items from dealers' point of view

Responses

Ranks	*Urban No. %age*	*Rural No. %age*	*Urban No. %age*	*Rural No. %age*	*Urban No. %age*	*Rural No. %age*	*Urban No. %age*	*Rural No. %age*	*Total* *Urban No. %age*	*Total* *Rural No. %age*
I	52	34	32	26	28	16	6	6	118	82
	44.07	41.46	27.12	31.71	23.73	19.51	5.08	7.32	25.00	25.00
II	26	22	42	8	20	26	30	26	118	82
	22.03	26.83	35.59	9.76	16.95	31.71	25.42	31.71	25.00	25.00
III	18	12	30	32	40	14	12	22	100	80
	15.25	14.63	25.42	39.02	33.90	17.07	10.17	26.83	21.19	24.39
IV	16	14	4	6	20	24	38	6	78	50
	13.56	17.07	3.39	7.32	16.95	29.27	32.20	7.32	16.53	15.24
N.R	6	0	10	10	10	2	32	22	58	34
	5.08	0.00	8.47	12.20	8.47	2.44	27.12	26.83	12.29	10.37
Total	118	82	118	82	118	82	118	82	472	328

Income Group
(i) Income below 2000 P.M
(ii) Income from 2001 to 4000 P.M
(iii) Income from 4001 to 6000 P.M
(iv) Income above 6000 P.M
Source : As per the survey conducted

Table 4.9

Responses Regarding Reasons for Purchasing Ration Items from the Dealers' Point of view

Ranks	Urban No. %age	Rural No. %age	Urban No. %age	Rural No. %age	Urban No. %age	Rural No. %age	Total Urban No. %age	Total Rural No. %age
I	64 54.24	46 58.10	32 27.12	32 33.02	22 18.64	4 4.88	118 33.33	82 33.33
II	22 18.64	18 21.95	62 52.54	30 36.59	30 25.42	34 41.46	114 32.20	82 33.33
III	26 22.03	16 19.51	18 15.25	20 24.39	54 45.76	38 46.34	98 27.68	74 30.08
N.R	6 5.08	2 2.44	6 5.08	0 0.00	12 10.17	6 7.32	24 6.78	8 3.25
Total	118	82	118	82	118	82	354	246

Reasons

(i) Lower Price

(ii) Easy availability

(iii) Good quality

Source : As per the survey conducted

Responses have also been generated regarding selling packed products under the PDS. As Table 4.10 exhibits, 49.15 per cent respondents of the urban areas and 29.27 per cent of the rural areas are willing to sell the packed products not only for the convenience of the people but also for themselves. 57.63 per cent respondents of the urban areas are also of the opinion that they want to deal in a larger range of products supplied under the PDS whereas 51.22 per cent dealers of the rural areas are against this proposal. The responses are exhibited in Table 4.11.

Table 4.10
Response Regarding Selling Packed Products

Responses	*Urban*		*Rural*		*Total*	
	No. of Resp.	*%age*	*No. of Resp.*	*%age*	*No. of Resp.*	*%age*
Yes	58	49.15	24	29.27	82	41.00
No	32	27.12	44	53.66	76	38.00
To Some Extent	28	23.73	14	17.07	42	21.00
Total	118	100.00	82	100.00	200	100.00

Source : As per the survey conducted

Table 4.11
Response Regarding Dealing in a Larger Range of Products

Responses	*Urban*		*Rural*		*Total*	
	No. of Resp.	*%age*	*No. of Resp.*	*%age*	*No. of Resp.*	*%age*
Yes	68	57.63	40	48.78	108	54.00
No	50	42.37	42	51.22	92	46.00
No Response	–	–	–	–	–	–
Total	118	100.00	82	100.00	200	100.00

Source : As per the survey conducted

(ix) Age-Profile of Fair Price Shops :

Figures on the age-profile of fair price shops indicate how well established the dealers are. The profile also provides an idea of the number of shops that are new or only a few years old which may at times indicate the pace of the licensing process, and the so called 'mortality rate' of FPS. This can be treated as an important indicator of viability in the sense that persistent non-viability leads to the closure of the retail outlet.

At the regional level, the general tendency observed for both the urban and the rural areas is that a large proportion of outlets are more than five to eight years old. This may be indicative of a rapid rise in licensing during recent years and also as a consequence of the emphasis on licensing new outlets under the 20-point programme.

(x) Transport Costs of FPS :

Transport costs constitute an important component in the overall costs of running of PDS outlet. It varies with the location of the FPS in inaccessible areas, where it often founds to be very high. Transport costs are usually met by the dealers and depend largely on the distance to the wholesale depots. The transport cost of rural shops for all commodities is higher than that for the urban shops. This is because most of the rural FPSs are often located in far-flung areas and their access to wholesale depots is poor as compared to the urban shops. In Jammu Region, deliveries are made at the shop floor in order to overcome the time and cost constraints faced by retail dealers, but it seems that these delivery arrangements can be equally irregular and stand in need of proper review and planning.

(xi) Control and Regulation of FPS by Civil Supplies Authorities

The main thrust of all the rules, regulations, terms and conditions, under which the FPS makes supplies to the public, is to ensure that the consumers get what the government plans to provide at a fixed price in specified quantities and at fixed intervals of time. Generally, the terms and conditions of FPS authorisation have to be enforced by the department of civil supplies by means of inspection and checking of FPS and their records. Non-enforcement of the rules and regulations carries penalties including that of suspension and cancellation of FPS licence. For this purpose, the department has appointed Food Inspectors in the state. Thus, the administrative arrangements implemented with the help of enforcement staff like inspectors, work in the context of suitability and reasonableness of the rules and regulations for serving the objectives of the PDS.

(xii) Miscellaneous Factors :

A number of other factors connected with the administrative and organisational design of the PDS, particularly, in relation to FPS are important in determining the effectiveness of PDS.

(a) Non-fixity of scales :

The amount of goods which a consumer is entitled to buy from a FPS does not always remain fixed for a reasonably long period of time. On the basis of allotments received from the higher authorities, the district officials change the ration scales through administrative orders. Sometimes the changes in scales are announced in the newspapers and in radio. But the consumers do not come to know about the changes. Thus, the variability of scale, on the one hand, erodes the assurance of regular availability of a certain quantity of goods from the FPS and on the other hand, gives an opportunity to the unscrupulous dealer to mislead and defraud the consumers. The ability of consumers, therefore, to supplement his market purchases on a regular and assured basis from the FPS is weakened on account of non-fixity of scales.

(b) Role of Consumers :

Since dissemination of the information about the changes in ration-scales is not always easy and the unorganised consumer in his individual capacity does not have the time and resources to obtain and verify the necessary information, the relative power of the FPS dealer increases. This makes the position of the consumer vulnerable, more particularly in those cases in which the FPS dealer is able to induce the enforcement staff of the civil supply department to either collude with him or to condone his acts.

What follows from the discussion so far is that there exist a variety of rules, procedures, policies and administrative arrangements, which have evolved over the periods of time in an adhoc manner. Their significance in determining the viability and effectiveness of FPS as a means of serving the consumers and giving them fair and reasonable access to the PDS goods has not been consciously recognised and examined.

Chapter–5

The Consumer and the PDS

Any meaningful study of the PDS needs to focus its attention on the various factors that affect the degree of utilisation and the access for the consumer. In this chapter, an attempt has been made to examine the operational work of the public distribution system from the point of view of the consumers. The major focus of the analysis has been, first, on the consumers' attitude towards the PDS as such and second, on the procedural difficulties in the actual operation of the system. The procedural difficulties include the issuing of the ration cards, adequacy of the quantity supplied and quality of the goods, the timings of the supply and delays and the weighing procedure. An analysis of these factors would show an insight into not only the managerial aspects but an overall impact of the policy over the consumers.

For this purpose, 500 consumers, from both the Urban and the rural areas, have been surveyed. Thus, a major part of the study is related to the question of finding out the extent to which the PDS meets the essential consumption needs of the 'beneficiary' . Since Wheat, Rice and Sugar are the main commodities supplied under the PDS through out the country, the main concentration, therefore, is on these three commodities so as to find out the proportion of monthly requirements, of these respondent families, supplied through the PDS channels.

The sample particulars are as follows:

(a) Educational Qualifications:

Table 5.1 reveals that there are 1.08 per cent of the respondents in the Urban areas and 2.25 per cent respondents in the rural areas who are illiterate. The remaining percentages in the table show the literacy rate of the sample.

Table 5.1
Educational Level of Respondents

S No.	Education	Urban No.	Urban %	Rural No	Rural %	Total No.	Total %
1.	Illiterate	3	1.08	5	2.25	8	1.60
2.	Below Matric	15	5.39	26	11.71	41	8.20
3.	Matric	71	25.54	48	21.62	119	23.80
4.	Graduate	93	33.45	66	29.73	159	31.80
5.	Post Graduate	78	28.06	61	27.48	139	27.80
6.	Professional Courses	18	6.48	16	7.21	34	6.80
Total		278	100.00	222	100.00	500	100.00

Source : As per the survey conducted

(b) Occupation:

Table 5.2 shows the distribution of respondents according to occupation in both the Urban and the rural areas 43.16 per cent of the respondents in the Urban areas and 35.59 per cent of the respondents in the rural areas are in service. Rest of the percentages are self-explanatory.

Table 5.2
Occupation of the Respondents

S No.	Occupation	Urban No.	Urban %	Rural No.	Rural %	Total No.	Total %
1.	Student	64	23.02	46	20.72	110	22.00
2.	Service	120	43.16	79	35.59	199	39.80
3.	Business	47	16.91	38	17.12	85	17.00
4.	Agriculture	10	3.60	42	18.92	52	10.40
5.	Profession	32	11.51	11	4.95	43	8.60
6.	Any other	5	1.80	6	2.70	11	2.20
	Total	278	100.00	222	100.00	500	100.00

Source: As per the survey conducted

Figure 14(a)
Educational Level of Urban Respondents

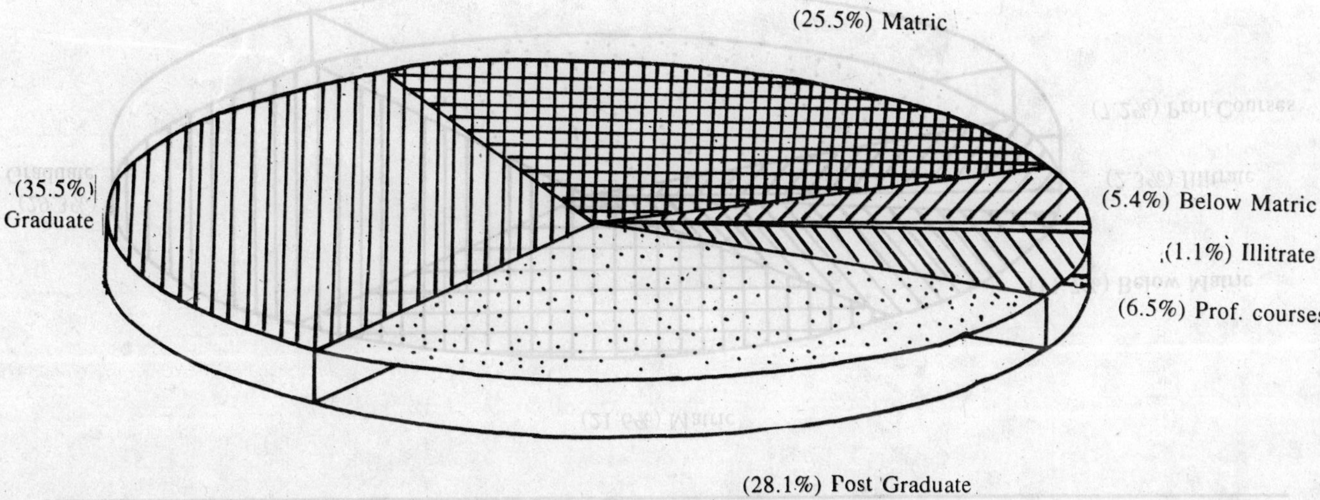

Figure 14(b)
Educational Level of Rural Respondents

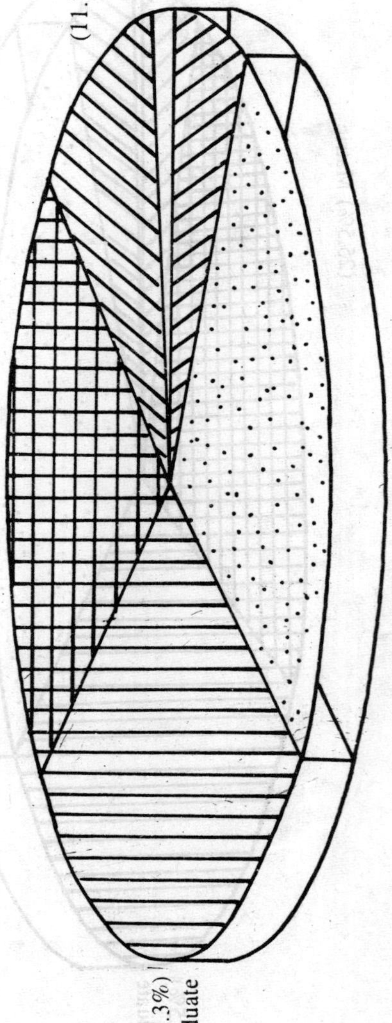

Figure 15(a)
Occupation of the Urban Respondents

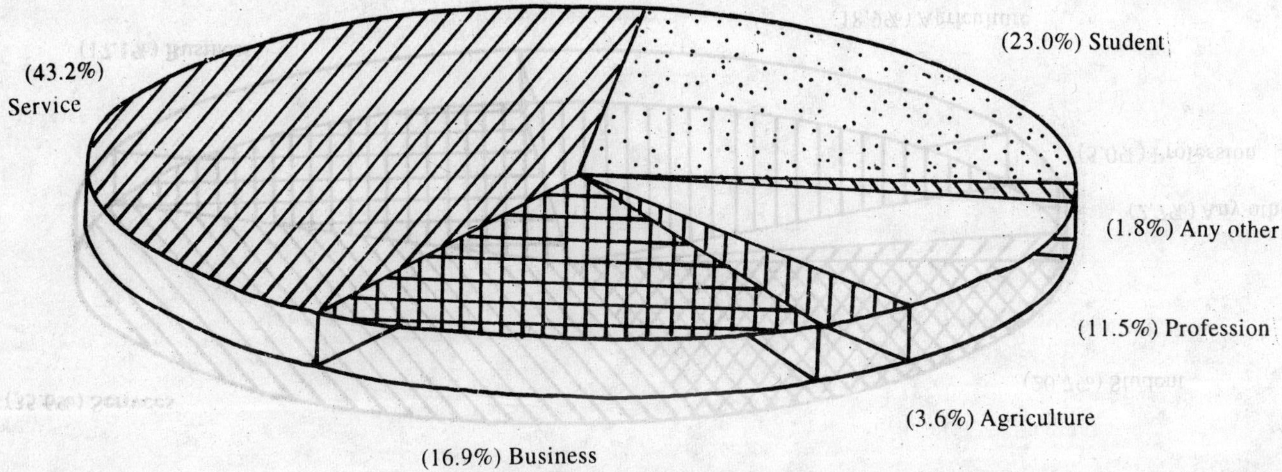

Figure 15(b)
Occupation of the Rural Respondents

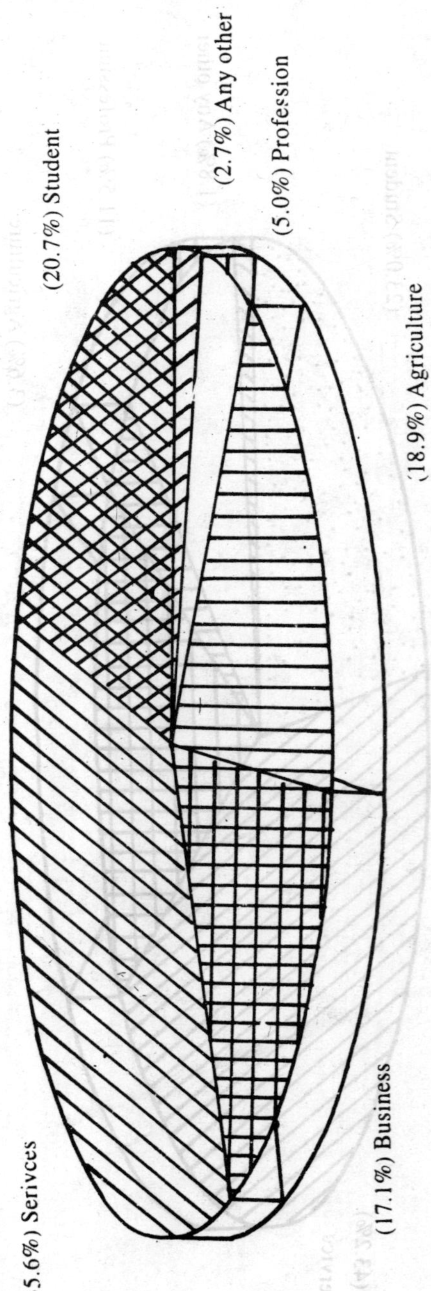

Figure 16(a)
Urban Respondents of Different Age Groups

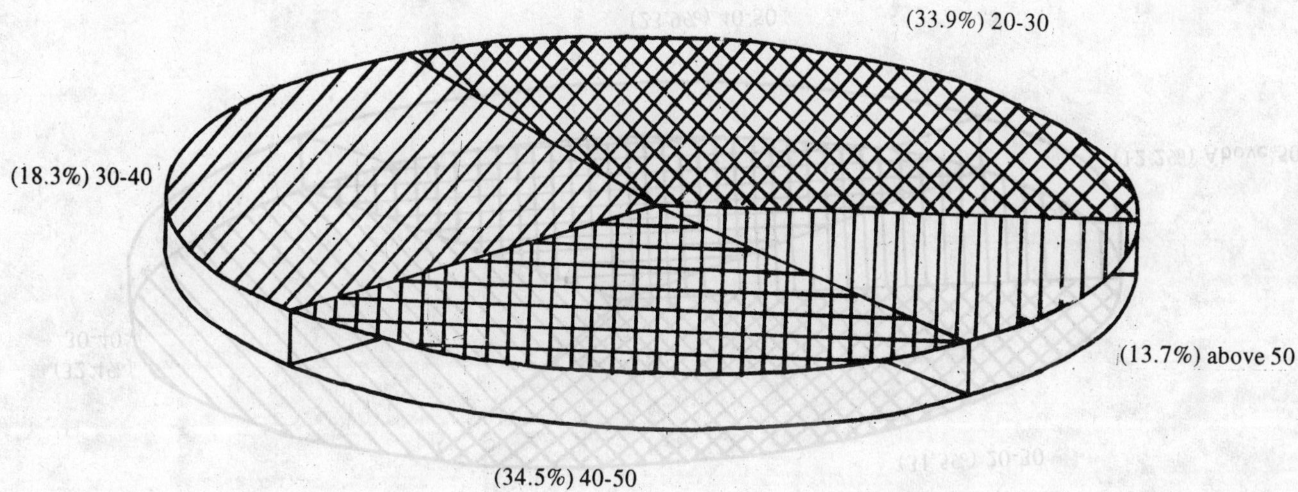

Figure 16(b)
Rural Respondents of Different Age Groups

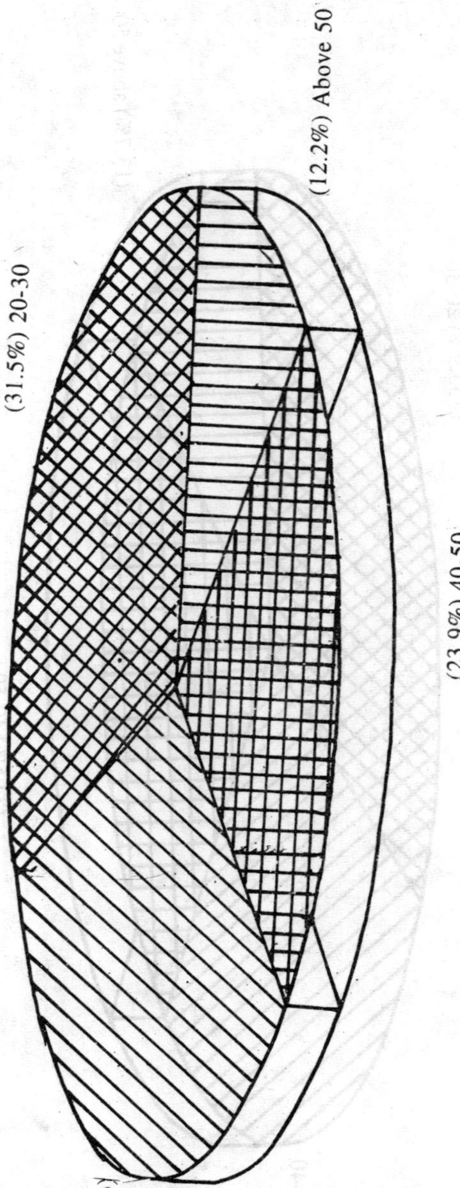

Figure 17(a)
Urban Respondents of Different Income Groups

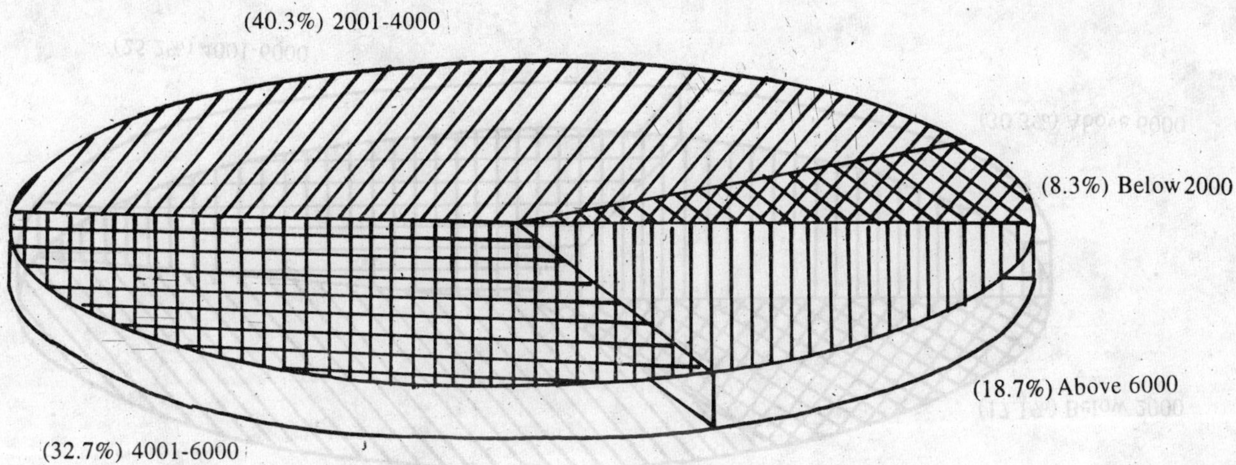

Figure 17(b)
Rural Respondents of Different Income Groups

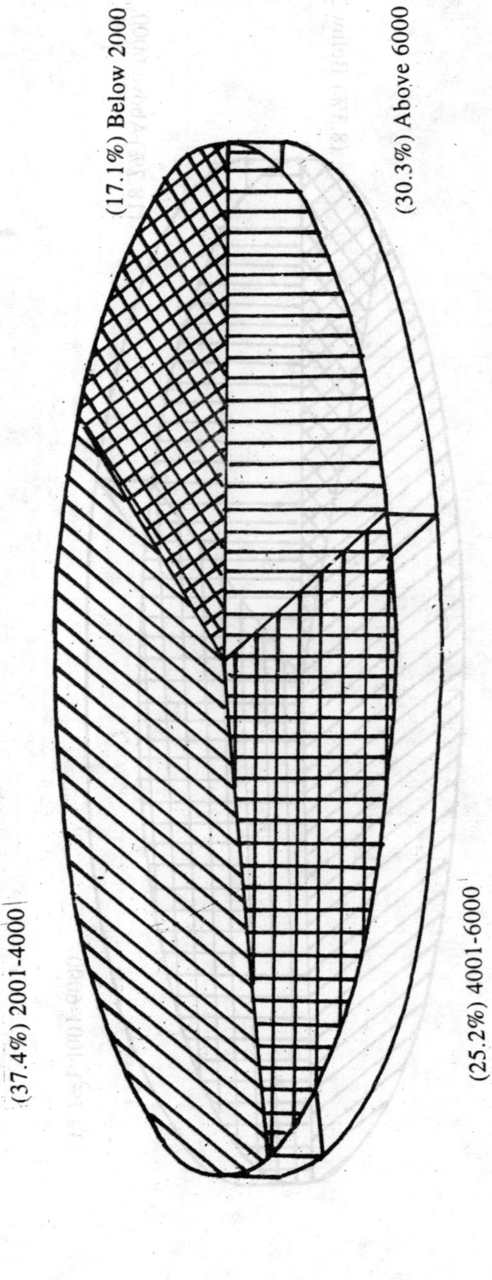

(c) Age:

The age composition of the respondents in Table 5.3 indicates that 61.87 per cent of the Urban respondents are of younger group, 24.46 per cent are of middle-age group and 13.67 per cent are 'above-50'. The sample from the rural areas presents almost the same picture of the age-group of the respondents.

Table 5.3
Respondents of Different Age Groups

S No.	*Age-Group*	*Urban* No.	%	*Rural* No.	%	*Total* No.	%
1.	20-30	93	33.45	70	31.53	163	32.60
2.	30-40	79	28.42	72	32.43	151	30.20
3.	40-50	68	24.46	53	23.88	121	24.20
4.	Above-50	38	13.67	27	12.16	65	13.00
	Total	278	100.00	222	100.00	500	100.00

Source : As per the survey conducted

(d) Income:

Table 5.4 indicates that 40.29 per cent respondents of the Urban areas and 37.39 per cent respondents of the rural areas fall in income group 'II' (Rs. 2,001-4,000). Low percentage of the respondents of income group 'I' (less than Rs. 2,000) shows that the people of this group are not able to purchase the items from the FPS on monthly basis because of their low monthly income which is also not fixed.

Table 5.4
Respondents of Different Income Group

S No.	*Income Group*	*Urban* No.	%	*Rural* No.	%	*Total* No.	%
1.	Below 2000	23	8.27	38	17.12	61	12.20
2.	2001-4000	112	40.29	83	37.39	195	39.00
3.	4001-6000	91	32.73	56	25.22	147	29.40
4.	Above 6000	52	18.71	45	20.27	97	19.40
Total		278	100.00	222	100.00	500	100.00

Source : As per the survey conducted

For collecting information from the households, different questions have been asked regarding consumption expenditure, quantities purchased, sources from which purchases are made etc.

An attempt has been made to know the awareness of the respondents with regard to the objectives of the PDS. The survey has revealed that the majority of the respondents of both the sectors are aware of the objectives of the Government in establishing the Fair Price Shops under the PDS. Table 5.5 depicts that the respondents have mentioned the objectives in the following order of importance by giving them ranks in ascending order:

(a) Supply of essential commodities,

(b) Proper distribution,

(c) To serve poor and vulnerable sections of the society,

(d) Price stability,

(e) Social service,

(f) Control of black marketing, etc.

Thus, the results show that irrespective of literacy, income and occupation, the awareness about the objectives of PDS is almost the same among the people of both the areas.

Table 5.6 shows that the respondents of both the Urban and the rural areas in the income groups "Rs. 2,001-4,000 and Rs. 4,001-6,000" are the real purchasers of the ration items. 44.64 per cent of the respondents of 'Income Group II' of the Urban areas and 38.55 per cent of the respondents of the same income group of the rural areas purchase and visit the FPSs occasionally. People, who never draw their ration quota from the FPS, are in majority in the 'Income Group-IV' because they do not have time to visit the FPS and they think that the quality of the food items is not good.

Table 5.7 shows that the respondents of the Urban and the rural areas have given the food items viz. wheat-flour, rice and sugar, the first, the second and the first ranks, respectively. It depicts that the majority of the respondents prefer to purchase the Wheat Flour and the sugar from the FPSs.

Responses have also been generated with regard to the distance between the residence and the FPS. Majority of the Urban and the rural respondents are of the view that the distance of the FPS from their residences is less than 1/2 Km. and they do not have any problem to reach their respective FPSs. The other results are shown in Table 5.8.

It has also been observed during the survey that the majority of the respondents are satisfied with the location of their FPS i.e., 71.22 per cent of the Urban respondents and 50.45 per cent of the rural respondents have said this as shown in Table 5.9. 49.55 per cent of the rural respondents and 28.78 per cent of the Urban respondents are not satisfied with the location of the FPSs. In the Urban and the rural areas, the respondents have given first rank i.e. 47.05 per cent and 50.00 per cent respectively to the reason 'distant location'.

The other reason 'location is unhygienic' has been awarded second rank in maximum number i.e. 35.00 per cent by the Urban respondents whereas the rural respondents have given it third rank in maximum number i.e. 29.09 percent. Rest of the percentages in the table are self-explanatory.

The respondents have also been asked if the commodities supplied under the PDS by the FPSs are available in time. In response to the question, the majority of the respondents have indicated that the food items are available in time and those who have given negative responses are of the opinion that the non-availability of the items is due to various reasons. Table 5.10 explains that there is a slight difference between

Table 5.5
Responses Generated Regarding Objectives of the Government in Establishing FPS under the PDS Objectives

	(i)		(ii)		(iii)		(iv)	
Ranks	*Urban* *No.* *%age*	*Rural* *No.* *%age*	*Urban* *No.* *%age*	*Rural* *No.* *%age*	*Urban* *No.* *%age*	*Rural* *No.* *%age*	*Urban* *No.* *%age*	*Rural* *No.* *%age*
I	94	64	32	28	33	38	36	27
	33.81	28.83	11.51	12.61	11.87	17.12	12.95	12.16
II	66	45	59	49	28	26	45	28
	23.74	20.27	21.22	22.07	10.07	11.71	16.19	12.61
III	56	38	63	49	31	32	21	16
	20.14	17.12	22.66	22.07	11.15	14.41	7.55	7.21
IV	14	23	49	34	41	29	42	49
	5.04	10.36	17.63	15.32	14.75	13.06	15.11	22.07
V	13	18	20	14	44	31	44	37
	4.68	8.11	7.19	6.31	15.83	13.96	15.83	16.67
VI	9	14	15	22	48	23	34	23
	3.24	6.31	5.40	9.91	17.27	10.36	12.23	10.36
VII	12	8	17	14	38	27	36	25
	4.32	3.60	6.12	6.31	13.67	12.16	12.95	11.26
VIII	0	0	0	0	0	0	0	0
	0.00	0.00	0.00	0.00	0.00	0.00	0.00	0.00
N.R	14	12	23	12	15	16	20	17
	5.04	5.41	8.27	5.41	5.40	7.21	7.19	7.66
Total	278	222	278	222	278	222	278	222

OBJECTIVES

(i) Supply of essential commodities

(ii) To serve poor people

(iii) Social service

(iv) Proper distribution

Table 5.5 (Continued)

Responses Generated Regarding Objectives of the Government in Establishing FPS under the PDS Objectives

(v)		(vi)		(vii)		(viii)		Total	
Urban No. %age	Rural No. %age	Urban No. %age	Rural No. %age	Urban No. %age	Rural No. %age	Urban No. %age	Rural No. %age	Urban No. %age	Rural No. %age
18	10	24	24	41	31	0	0	278	222
6.47	4.50	8.63	10.81	14.75	13.96	0.00	0.00	12.50	12.50
14	30	30	24	24	20	12	0	278	222
5.04	13.51	10.79	10.81	8.63	9.01	4.32	0.00	12.50	12.50
30	24	26	36	40	22	6	2	273	219
10.79	10.81	9.35	16.22	14.39	9.91	2.16	0.90	12.28	12.33
38	30	48	12	28	22	4	5	264	204
13.67	13.51	17.27	5.41	10.07	9.91	1.44	2.25	11.87	11.49
62	42	38	28	37	20	2	2	260	192
22.30	18.92	13.67	12.61	13.31	9.01	0.72	0.90	11.69	10.81
58	24	48	48	30	26	0	0	242	180
20.86	10.81	17.27	21.62	10.79	11.71	0.00	0.00	10.88	10.14
42	44	42	30	54	41	0	0	241	189
15.11	19.82	15.11	13.51	19.42	18.47	0.00	0.00	10.84	10.64
0	0	0	0	0	0	1	0	1	0
0.00	0.00	0.00	0.00	0.00	0.00	0.36	0.00	0.04	0.00
16	18	22	20	24	40	253	213	387	348
5.76	8.11	7.91	9.01	8.63	18.02	91.01	95.95	17.40	19.59
278	222	278	222	278	222	278	222	2224	1776

(v) Avoid middlemen

(vi) Price stability

(vii) Controlloing black marketing

(viii) Any other

Source : As per the survey conducted

Table 5.6
Responses Regarding Frequency of Purchasing Food Items from the FPS

Frequency of Purchasing	Income Group-I Less than Rs. 2000 No. of Resp. = 61				Income Group-II Rs. 2001 to Rs. 4000 No. of Resp. = 195				Income Group-III Rs. 4001 to 6000 No. of Resp. = 147				Income Group-IV Above Rs. 6000 No. of Resp. = 97				Total No. of Resp. Generated = 500			
	Urban		Rural		Urban		Rural		Urban		Rural		Urban		Rural		Urban		Rural	
	No. of Resp.	%age	No. of Resp.	%age	No. of Resp.	%age	No. of Resp.	%age	No. of Resp.	%age	No. of Resp.	%age	No. of Resp.	%age	No. of Resp.	%age	No. of Resp.	%age	No. of Resp.	%age
Regulary	12	52.17	25	65.79	60	53.57	45	54.22	53	58.24	8	14.29	34	65.38	2	4.44	159	57.20	80	36.60
Occassion	11	47.83	11	28.95	50	44.64	32	38.55	30	32.97	42	75.00	0	0.00	16	35.56	91	32.73	101	45.50
Never	0	0.00	2	5.26	2	1.79	6	7.23	8	8.79	6	10.71	18	34.62	27	60.00	28	10.07	41	15.00
Total	23	100.00	38	100.00	112	100.00	83	100.00	91	100.00	56	100.00	52	100.00	45	100.00	278	100.00	222	100.00

Source : As per Survey Conducted.

Table 5.7
Responses Regarding Purchasing Items mainly from the FPS

Items	Wheat/Wheat Flour				Rice				Sugar				Total			
	Urban		Rural		Urban		Rural		Urban		Rural		Urban		Rural	
	No. of Resp.	%age	No. of Resp.	%age	No. of Resp.	%age	No. of Resp.	%age	No. of Resp.	%age	No. of Resp.	%age	No. of Resp.	%age	No. of Resp.	%age
I	123	45.06	77	36.16	47	17.22	33	15.49	103	37.73	103	48.36	273	33.33	213	33.33
II	96	35.16	72	33.80	114	41.76	82	38.50	60	21.98	55	25.82	270	32.97	209	32.71
III	48	17.58	49	23.00	101	37.00	94	44.13	94	34.43	49	23.00	243	29.67	192	30.05
N.R	6	2.20	15	7.04	11	4.02	4	1.88	16	5.86	6	2.82	33	4.03	25	3.91
Total	273	100.00	213	100.00	273	100.00	213	100.00	273	100.00	213	100.00	819	100.00	639	100.00

No. of resp. generated (Urban = 278-5 = 273)

No. of resp. generated (Rural = 222-9 = 213)

Source : As per the survey conducted

the responses of both the Urban and the rural respondents regarding the reasons like 'irregular supply from the government itself, transport problems, 'storage problems', carelessness on the part of the dealers', 'black-marketing' etc.

Table 5.8
Responses Generated Regarding Distance between the Residence and the FPS

S No.	Distance	Urban		Rural		Total	
		No.	%	No.	%	No.	%
1.	Less than 1/2 km	167	60.08	84	37.84	251	5.02
2.	Less than 1 km	78	28.05	60	27.03	138	27.60
3.	Less than 2km	22	7.92	50	22.52	72	14.40
4.	Above 2 km	11	3.95	28	12.61	39	7.80
	Total	278	100.00	222	100.00	500	100.00

Source : As per the survey conducted

Responses have also been generated with regard to satisfaction with the weighing process in the FPS in Table 5.11. Some of the respondents from both the areas give negative responses due to various reasons, which they think, are the main reasons of dissatisfaction. First rank is given by 53.19 per cent of the Urban respondents to the reason 'intentional under weighing' and 51.43 per cent of the rural respondents, too, have given the same rank to the same reason. 'Weights and measures are not as per the rules' has gained third and second rank by the respondents of both the areas. Again, the second rank by the Urban respondents and the third rank by the rural respondents are given to the third reason which shows that the weighing process differs not only from person to person but also from place to place.

The question is also asked about the time consumption to draw ration from the FPS. Table 5.12 depicts that the majority of the Urban and the rural respondents have said that '1/2-1 hour' is spent in purchasing the ration items from the FPSs.

Table 5.9
Responses Generated Regarding Satisfaction with the Location of FPS

	Response			
	Urban		Rural	
	No	%age	No	%age
Yes	198	71.22	112	50.45
No	80	28.78	110	49.55
N.R	0	0.00	0	0.00
Total	278	100.00	222	100.00

If No, the Reasons of Dissatisfaction

	Distant Location				Location is Unhygenic				Not Suitable for Ladies				Any Other				Total			
	Urban		Rural		Urban		Rural		Urban		Rural		Urban		Rural		Urban		Rural	
Ranks	No	%age	No	%age	No	%age	No	%age	No	%age	No	%age	No	%age	No	%age	No	%age	No	%age
I	38	47.50	55	50.00	15	18.75	31	28.18	16	20.00	18	16.36	11	13.75	6	5.46	80	25.00	110	25.00
II	15	18.75	28	25.45	28	35.00	31	28.18	24	30.00	35	31.82	13	16.25	11	10.00	80	25.00	105	23.86
III	24	30.00	13	11.82	22	27.50	32	29.09	28	35.00	45	40.92	5	6.25	8	7.27	79	24.69	98	22.27
IV	2	2.50	5	4.55	14	17.50	11	10.00	9	11.25	5	4.54	18	22.50	41	37.27	43	13.43	62	14.09
N.R	1	1.25	9	8.18	1	1.25	5	4.55	3	3.75	7	6.36	33	41.25	44	40.00	38	11.88	65	14.78
Total	80	100.00	110	100.00	80	100.00	110	100.00	80	100.00	110	100.00	80	100.00	110	100.00	320	100.00	440	100.00

Source : As per the survey conducted

Table 5.13 reveals the reasons for preference to purchase the ration items from the FPSs vis-a-vis the open market. The first reason 'lower price' has gained first preference for all the food items. First rank by the Urban respondents, second rank by the rural respondents to the 'Wheat/ Wheat Flour, fifth rank by the Urban respondents and second rank by the rural respondents to the 'rice' and third rank by the respondents of both the areas to the 'Sugar' have been given in maximum numbers. Rest of the percentages in the table show that there is a slight difference among the responses of the respondents of both the areas regarding the other reasons for preference.

The survey further reveals that the majority of the consumers (respondents) of both the areas prefer 'sugar' followed by 'wheat/wheat flour' and then 'rice'. The ranks given by the respondents belonging to different income groups are exhibited in Table 5.14. 'Sugar and' wheat flour are preferred by all income groups whereas 'rice' has been awarded second rank in maximum number by Income groups III and IV.

Thus, the study reveals that inspite of the constraints, a significant majority of both the Urban and the rural respondents have shown their preference for PDS. This is because in times of scarcities and shortages, this is the only system which provides them goods at fair prices. Further, the majority of the respondents in both the Urban and the rural sectors do not have adequate money to buy the commodities in the open market.

Table 5.10
Responses Generated Regarding Availability of Ration commodities in Time

Response	*Urban*		*Rural*	
	No.	*%*	*No.*	*%*
Yes	172	61.87	131	59.00
No	103	37.05	84	37.84
No Response	3	1.08	7	3.16
Total	278	100.00	20	100.00

If No, the Reasons

Ranks	Urban No. %age	Rural No. %age	Urban No. %age	Rural No. %age	Urban No. %age	Rural No. %age	Urban No. %age	Rural No. %age	Urban No. %age	Rural No. %age	Urban No. %age	Rural No. %age	Urban No. %age	Rural No. %age	Total Urban No. %age	Total Rural No. %age
I	20	18	12	10	16	13	18	16	16	12	9	7	12	8	103	84
	19.42	21.43	11.65	11.90	15.53	15.48	17.48	19.05	15.53	14.29	8.74	8.33	11.65	9.52	14.29	14.29
II	18	16	13	12	13	10	19	15	10	8	13	12	17	11	103	84
	17.48	19.05	12.62	14.29	12.62	11.90	18.45	17.86	9.71	9.52	12.62	14.29	16.50	13.10	14.29	14.29
III	18	14	11	6	10	8	12	9	19	16	13	12	20	19	103	84
	17.48	16.67	10.68	7.14	9.71	9.52	11.65	10.71	18.45	19.05	12.62	14.29	19.42	22.62	14.29	14.29
IV	10	9	17	15	11	10	15	12	13	10	12	10	15	13	93	79
	9.71	10.71	16.50	17.86	10.68	11.90	14.56	14.29	12.62	11.90	11.65	11.90	14.56	15.48	12.90	13.44
V	10	9	10	14	17	13	14	13	14	10	16	13	12	10	93	82
	9.71	10.71	9.71	16.67	16.50	15.48	13.59	15.48	13.59	11.90	15.53	15.48	11.65	11.90	12.90	13.95
VI	11	5	20	15	14	12	10	8	12	11	13	11	10	9	90	71
	10.68	5.95	19.42	17.86	13.59	14.29	9.71	9.52	11.65	13.10	12.62	13.10	9.71	10.71	12 48	12.07
VII	8	7	13	10	16	14	8	6	10	10	15	10	9	8	79	65
	7.77	8.33	12.62	11.90	15.53	16.67	7.77	7.14	9.71	11.90	14.56	11.90	8.74	9.52	10.96	11.05
N.R	8	6	7	2	6	4	7	5	9	7	12	9	8	6	57	39
	7.77	7.14	6.80	2.38	5.83	4.76	6.80	5.95	8.74	8.33	11.65	10.71	7.77	7.14	7.91	6.63
Total	103	84	103	84	103	84	103	84	103	84	103	84	103	84	721	588

Reasons *(i)* Irregular supply *(ii)* Transport problems *(iii)* Storage problems *(iv)* Carelessness of dealers *(v)* Black marketing *(vi)* Long queue *(vii)* Lack of Govt. supervision

Source : As per the survey conducted

Table 5.11

Responses Regarding Satisfaction with Weighing Process in FPS

Response	*Urban*		*Rural*	
	No	*%age*	*No*	*%age*
Yes	182	65.47	150	67.57
No	94	33.81	70	31.53
N.R	2	0.72	2	0.90
Total	278	100.00	222	100.00

If No, the Reasons of Dissatisfaction

	International Underweighing				*Weight & Measures are not as per rules*				*Weighing Method Varies*				*Any other*				*Total*			
Ranks No.	*Urban No.*	*%age*	*Rural No.*	*%age*	*Urban No.*	*%age*	*Rural No.*	*%age*	*Urban No.*	*%age*	*Rural No.*	*%age*	*Urban No.*	*%age*	*Rural No.*	*%age*	*Urban No.*	*%age*	*Rural No.*	*%age*
I	50	53.19	36	51.43	12	12.76	22	31.43	25	26.59	10	14.29	7	7.45	2	2.86	94	25	70	25
II	25	26.60	19	27.14	34	36.18	29	41.43	31	32.98	19	27.14	4	4.26	3	4.28	94	25	70	25
III	19	20.21	15	21.43	48	51.06	17	24.28	21	22.34	25	35.71	5	5.32	8	11.43	93	24.73	65	23.22
IV	0	0.00	0	0.00	0	0.00	0	0.00	13	13.83	10	14.29	12	12.76	4	5.72	25	6.65	14	5
N.R	0	0.00	0	0.00	0	0.00	2	2.86	4	4.26	6	8.57	66	70.21	53	75.71	70	18.62	61	21.78
Total	94	100.00	70	100.00	94	100.00	70	100.00	94	100.00	70	100.00	94	100.00	70	100.00	376	100	280	100

Source: As per the Survey Conducted

Table 5.12

Responses Regarding Time Consumption to Draw Ration from FPS

S No.	*Time*	*Urban* No.	%	*Rural* No.	%	*Total* No.	%
1.	Less than 1/2 Hr.	109	39.21	67	30.18	176	35.20
2.	1/2 Hr-1 Hr	123	44.24	110	49.55	233	46.60
3.	1-2 Hr	32	11.51	33	14.80	65	13.00
4.	Above 2 Hr	14	5.04	7	3.15	21	4.20
5.	No Response			5	2.26	5	1.00
Total		278	100.00	222	100.00	500	100.00

Source : As per the survey conducted

Table 5.15 shows the responses regarding the quantity of the ration items issued under the PDS. 75.18 per cent and 58.27 per cent of the Urban respondents and 66.22 per cent and 49.10 per cent of the rural respondents are of the opinion that the quantity of both the wheat flour and rice, respectively are quite sufficient whereas the majority of respondents of both the areas are of the view that the sugar quota is not sufficient. It does not meet their requirement. Responses have also been generated regarding the basis for issuing ration quota for all the food items.

Table 5.16 depicts that 41.00 per cent of the Urban respondents are of the opinion that both the size and the income of the family should be the basis for issuing ration quota to each family whereas 40.99 per cent of the rural respondents do not agree with this statement. According to them, the basis should be only the size of the family.

Regarding the quality of the commodities supplied by the PDS in both the Urban and the rural sectors, majority of the respondents have said that the quality of all the food items

Table 5.13

Responses Regarding the Reasons for Preference to Purchase Food Items from the FPS than Open Market

Ranks	*Low Price*		*High Quality*		*Good Taste*		*Nutritive Value*		*Easy Digestable*		*Easy Available*		*Total*	
	Urban No. *%age*	*Rural* No. *%age*	*Urban* No. *%age*	*Rural* No. *%age*	*Urban* No. *%age*	*Rural* No. *%age*	*Urban* No. *%age*	*Rural* No. *%age*	*Urban* No. *%age*	*Rural* No. *%age*	*Urban* No. *%age*	*Rural* No. *%age*	*Urban* No. *%age*	*Rural* No. *%age*
I	97	80	59	41	35	25	32	40	30	26	25	10	278	222
	34.89	36.04	21.22	18.47	12.59	11.26	11.51	18.02	10.79	11.71	8.99	4.50	16.67	16.67
Wheat/ II	68	43	78	51	61	46	43	37	13	37	15	8	278	222
Wheat	24.46	19.37	28.06	22.97	21.94	20.72	15.47	16.67	4.68	16.67	5.40	3.60	16.67	16.67
Flour III	40	38	49	37	52	44	46	36	46	25	45	42	278	222
	14.39	17.12	17.63	16.67	18.71	19.82	16.55	16.22	16.55	11.26	16.19	18.92	16.67	16.67
No. of IV	33	20	28	24	53	58	54	44	70	54	37	20	275	220
Resp.	11.87	9.01	10.07	10.81	19.06	26.13	19.42	19.82	25.18	24.32	13.31	9.01	16.49	16.52
V	30	19	24	25	40	20	62	37	51	32	69	60	276	193
U = 278	10.79	8.56	8.63	11.26	14.39	9.01	22.30	16.67	18.35	14.41	24.82	27.03	16.55	14.49
R = 222 VI	6	10	30	28	27	15	28	12	45	36	60	58	196	159
	2.16	4.50	10.79	12.61	9.71	6.76	10.07	5.41	16.19	16.22	21.58	26.13	11.75	11.94
N.R	4	12	10	16	10	14	13	16	23	12	27	24	87	94
	1.44	5.41	3.60	7.21	3.60	6.31	4.68	7.21	8.27	5.41	9.71	10.81	5.22	7.06
Total	278	222	278	222	278	222	278	222	278	222	278	222	1668	1332

Table (Continued. . .)

Responses Regarding the Reasons for Preference to Purchase Food Items from the FPS than Open Market

	Ranks	Low Price		High Quality		Good Taste		Nutritive Value		Easy Digestable		Easy Available		Total	
		Urban No. %age	Rural No. %age	Urban No. %age	Rural No. %age	Urban No. %age	Rural No. %age	Urban No. %age	Rural No. %age	Urban No. %age	Rural No. %age	Urban No. %age	Rural No. %age	Urban No. %age	Rural No. %age
	I	98	58	27	23	26	29	24	20	35	33	40	37	250	200
Rice		39.20	29.00	10.80	11.50	10.40	14.50	9.60	10.00	14.00	16.50	16.00	18.50	16.67	16.67
	II	52	47	50	48	38	26	34	33	38	31	38	15	250	200
		20.80	23.50	20.00	24.00	15.20	13.00	13.60	16.50	15.20	15.50	15.20	7.50	16.67	16.67
No. of	III	36	34	49	44	43	42	49	42	36	30	37	8	250	200
Resp.		14.40	17.00	19.60	22.00	17.20	21.00	19.60	21.00	14.40	15.00	14.80	4.00	16.67	16.67
U = 250	IV	29	29	32	31	52	47	56	41	49	35	28	7	246	190
R = 200		11.60	14.50	12.80	15.50	20.80	23.50	22.40	20.50	19.60	17.50	11.20	3.50	16.40	15.83
	V	15	16	53	30	30	21	40	34	41	31	48	46	227	178
		6.00	8.00	21.20	15.00	12.00	10.50	16.00	17.00	16.40	15.50	19.20	23.00	15.13	14.83
	VI	12	11	29	17	34	29	29	14	26	23	30	45	160	139
		4.80	5.50	11.60	8.50	13.60	14.50	11.60	7.00	10.40	11.50	12.00	22.50	10.67	11.58
	N.R	8	5	10	7	27	6	18	16	25	17	29	42	117	93
		3.20	2.50	4.00	3.50	10.80	3.00	7.20	8.00	10.00	8.50	11.60	21.00	7.80	7.75
	Total	250	200	250	200	250	200	250	200	250	200	250	200	1500	1200

Table (Continued . . .)

Responses Regarding the Reasons for Preference to Purchase Food Items from the FPS than Open Market

		Low Price		High Quality		Good Taste		Nutritive Value		Easy Digestable		Easy Available		Total	
	Ranks	Urban No. %Age	Rural No. %Age	Urban No. %Age	Rural No. %Age	Urban No. %Age	Rural No. %Age	Urban No. %Age	Rural No. %Age	Urban No. %Age	Rural No. %Age	Urban No. %Age	Rural No. %Age	Urban No. %Age	Rural No. %Age
	I	96	80	40	37	42	31	34	31	31	25	25	6	268	210
Sugar		35.82	38.10	14.93	17.62	15.67	14.76	12.69	14.76	11.57	11.90	9.33	2.86	16.67	16.67
	II	58	46	41	30	42	40	37	29	40	29	50	36	268	210
No. of		21 64	21.90	15.30	14.29	15.67	19.05	13.81	13.81	14.93	13.81	18.66	17.14	16.67	16.67
Resp.	III	37	31	58	51	56	43	39	40	34	30	44	15	268	210
		13.81	14.76	21.64	24.29	20.90	20.48	14.55	19.05	12.69	14.29	16.42	7.14	16.67	16.67
U = 268	IV	26	20	53	44	52	46	63	52	29	29	35	15	258	206
R = 210		9.70	9.52	19.78	20.95	19.40	21.90	23.51	24.76	10.82	13.81	13.06	7.14	16.04	16.35
	V	19	11	26	24	31	24	38	25	56	44	30	30	200	158
		7.09	5.24	9.70	11.43	11.57	11.43	14.18	11.90	20.90	20.95	11.19	14.29	12.44	12.54
	VI	17	12	29	14	24	13	28	19	47	30	60	56	205	144
		6.34	5.71	10.82	6.67	8.96	6.19	10.45	9.05	17.54	14.29	22.39	26.67	12.75	11.43
	N.R	15	10	21	10	21	13	29	14	31	23	24	52	141	122
		5.60	4.76	7.84	4.76	7.84	6.19	10.82	6.67	11.57	10.95	8.96	24.76	8.77	9.68
	Total	268	210	268	210	268	210	268	210	268	210	268	210	1608	1260

is average and this is shown in Table 5.17. Thus, there are very few people who have said about the bad quality of the goods supplied through PDS. Thus, it can be inferred that a significant majority of the respondents in both the Urban and the rural sectors have not made any complaint seriously about the quality of the above-mentioned commodities.

With regard to the price of the controlled items, majority of the respondents of both the sectors have expressed their satisfaction. Those respondents who are not satisfied with the pricing system of the commodities supplied under the PDS have given reasons for dissatisfaction. As Table 5.18 explains, the reason 'no credit facilities' is awarded with the second rank by the respondents of both the areas whereas the administered price of 'Sugar' is considered to be very high. Other reasons are also given by the respondents in this respect.

The respondents are also asked to rate the behaviour of the ration shop dealer with the customers. Table 5.19 explains that 50.36 per cent of the Urban respondents and 40.99 per cent of the rural respondents have rated the behaviour of the FPS dealer as courteous. The percentage of the respondents, who have rated the behaviour of the dealer as indifferent and rude, is more in the rural sector as compared to that of the Urban sector. This clearly indicates that the PDS lacks the business culture and is not service-oriented as expected of a public agency.

Table 5.14
Responses Regarding Consumer Preference for Different Food Items

Ranks	*Income Group-I (Less than Rs. 2000) No. of Response = 61*				*Income Group-II (Rs. 2001 to 4000) No. of Response = 195*				*Income Group-III (Rs. 4001 to 6000) No. of Responses = 147*				*Income Group-IV (above Rs. 6000) No. of Responses = 97*				*Total No. of Responses = 500*			
	Urban		*Rural*		*Urban*		*Rural*		*Urban*		*Rural*		*Urban*		*Rural*		*Urban*		*Rural*	
	No	*%age*	*No*	*%age*	*No*	*%age*	*No*	*%age*	*No*	*%age*	*No*	*%age*	*No*	*%age*	*No*	*%age*	*No*	*%age*	*No*	*%age*
I	10	43.48	13	34.21	45	40.18	30	36.14	39	42.86	27	48.21	18	34.62	23	51.11	112	40.29	93	41.89
II	9	39.13	11	28.95	38	33.93	27	32.53	25	27.47	15	26.79	16	30.76	10	22.22	88	31.65	63	28.37
III	3	13.04	9	23.68	22	19.64	18	21.69	23	25.27	11	19.64	15	28.85	9	20.00	63	22.66	47	21.18
N.R	1	4.35	5	13.16	7	6.25	8	9.64	4	4.40	3	5.36	3	5.77	3	6.67	15	5.40	19	8.56
Total	23	100.00	38	100	112	100	83	100	91	100	56	100	52	100.00	45	100	278	100	222	100

Ranks	*Income Group-I (Less than Rs. 2000) No. of Response = 61*				*Income Group-II (Rs. 2001 to 4000) No. of Response = 195*				*Income Group-III (Rs. 4001 to 6000) No. of Responses = 147*				*Income Group-IV (above Rs. 6000) No. of Responses = 97*				*Total No. of Responses = 500*			
	Urban		*Rural*		*Urban*		*Rural*		*Urban*		*Rural*		*Urban*		*Rural*		*Urban*		*Rural*	
	No	*%age*	*No*	*%age*	*No*	*%age*	*No*	*%age*	*No*	*%age*	*No*	*%age*	*No*	*%age*	*No*	*%age*	*No*	*%age*	*No*	*%age*
I	13	56.52	25	65.79	30	26.79	33	39.76	30	32.97	25	44.64	21	40.38	13	28.89	94	33.81	96	43.24
II	10	43.48	12	31.58	53	47.32	31	37.35	33	36.26	31	55.36	29	55.77	25	55.56	125	44.96	99	44.59
III	0	0.00	1	2.63	21	18.75	15	18.07	21	23.08	0	0.00	0	0.00	5	11.11	42	15.11	21	9.46
N.R	0	0.00	0	0.00	8	7.14	4	4.82	7	7.69	0	0.00	2	3.85	2	4.44	17	6.12	6	2.71
Total	23	100.00	38	100	112	100	83	100	91	100	56	100	52	100.00	45	100	278	100	222	100

Table : 5.14
Responses Regarding Cosumer Preferece for Different Food Items

Ranks	Income Group-I (Less than Rs. 2000) No. of Response = 61				Income Group-II (Rs. 2001 to 4000) No. of Response = 195				Income Group-III (Rs. 4001 to 6000) No. of Responses = 147				Income Group-IV (above Rs. 6000) No. of Responses = 97				Total No. of Responses = 500			
	Urban		Rural		Urban		Rural		Urban		Rural		Urban		Rural		Urban		Rural	
	No	%Age	No	%Age	No	%Age	No	%Age	No	%Age	No	%Age	No	%Age	No	%Age	No	%Age	No	%Age
I	18	78.26	25	65.79	58	51.79	35	42.17	44	48.35	32	57.14	30	57.69	35	77.78	150	53.96	127	57.21
II	5	21.74	11	28.95	30	26.79	26	31.32	37	40.66	15	26.79	22	42.31	10	22.22	94	33.81	62	27.93
III	0	0.00	2	5.26	22	19.64	18	21.69	10	10.99	9	16.07	0	0.00	0	0.00	32	11.51	29	13.06
N.R	0	0.00	0	0.00	2	1.78	4	4.82	0	0.00	0	0.00	0	0.00	0	0.00	2	0.72	4	1.80
TOTAL	23	100.00	38	100	112	100	83	100	91	100	56	100	52	100.00	45	100	278	100	222	100

SOURCE : AS PER THE SURVEY CONDUCTED

TABLE : 5.15

Responses Regarding Quantity of the Ration Items Issued under the PDS

Response	(i) *Wheat/Wheat Flor* *Urban*		*Rural*		(ii) *Rice* *Urban*		*Rural*		(iii) *Sugar* *Urban*		*Rural*	
	No. of Resp.	*%Age*	*No. of Resp.*	*%Age*	*No. of Resp.*	*%Age*	*No. of Resp.*	*% Age*	*No. of Resp*	*%Age*	*No. of Resp*	*%Age*
Sufficient	209	75.18	147	66.22	162	58.27	109	49.10	92	33.09	58	26.13
In-Sufficiet	59	21.22	61	27.48	113	40.65	95	42.79	180	64.75	150	67.57
N.R.	10	3.60	14	6.30	3	1.08	18	8.11	6	2.16	14	6.30
Total	278	100.00	222	100.00	278	100.00	222	100.00	278	100.00	222	100.00

Source : As per the Survey Conducted

Table 5.16
Responses Regarding basis for Issuing Ration Quota

S No.	BASE	Urban No.	Urban %	Rural No.	Rural %	Total No.	Total %
1.	Size of Family	96	34.53	91	40.99	187	37.40
2.	Income	66	23.74	59	26.58	125	25.00
3.	Both	114	41.00	71	31.98	185	37.00
6.	No Resp.	2	0.73	1	0.45	3	0.06
	Total	278	100.00	222	100.00	500	100.00

Source : As per the survey conducted.

Table 5.17
Responses Regarding Quality of the Food Items Issued under the PDS

	(i) Wheat/Wheat Flor				(ii) Rice				(iii) Sugar			
	Urban		*Rural*		*Urban*		*Rural*		*Urban*		*Rural*	
se	*No. of Resp.*	*%age*	*No. of Resp.*	*%age*	*No. of Resp.*	*%age*	*No. of Resp.*	*% age*	*No. of Resp*	*%age*	*No. of Resp*	*%age*
	100	35.97	79	35.58	58	20.86	59	26.58	96	34.53	75	33.78
e	138	49.64	107	48.20	126	45.32	107	48.20	136	48.92	87	39.19
	40	14.39	36	16.22	94	33.82	56	25.22	46	16.55	60	27.03
	278	100.00	222	100.00	278	100.00	222	100.00	278	100.00	222	100.00

Table 5.18

Responses Regardings Satisfaction with Pricing System

Response

	Urban		Rural	
	No	%age	No	%age
Yes	181	65.11	126	56.76
No.	91	32.73	81	36.49
N.R.	6	2.16	15	6.75
Total	278	100.00	222	100.00

If No, The Reasons of Dissatisfaction

	(i) No Credit Facilities				(ii) ADM. Price of Sugar is high				(iii) Any Other				Total			
	Urban		Rural		Urban		Rural		Urban		Rural		Urban		Rural	
	No	%age	No	%age	No	%age	No	%age	No	%age	No	%age	No	%age	No	%age
I	29	31.87	19	23.46	48	52.75	31	38.27	14	15.38	31	38.27	91	33.33	81	33.33
II	44	48.35	44	54.32	31	34.06	25	30.86	14	15.38	11	13.58	89	32.6	80	32.93
III	12	13.19	12	14.81	11	12.09	23	28.39	24	26.38	20	24.69	47	17.22	55	22.63
N.R.	6	6.59	6	7.41	1	1.1	2	2.48	39	42.86	19	23.46	46	16.85	27	11.12
Total	91	100.00	81	100.00	91	100.00	81	100.00	91	100.00	81	100.00	273	100.00	243	100.00

Source : As per the survey conducted.

Table 5.19

Responses Regarding Rating the Behaviour of FPS Dealers

S No.	Behaviour	Urban No.	Urban %	Rural No.	Rural %	Total No.	Total %
1.	Courteous	140	50.36	91	40.99	231	46.20
2.	Indifferent	80	28.78	77	34.68	157	31.40
3.	Rude	49	17.62	46	20.73	95	19.00
4.	No Response	9	3.24	8	3.60	17	3.40
	Total	278	100.00	222	100.00	500	100.00

Source : As per the survey conducted

Table 5.20 depicts that 48.20 per cent of the Urban respondents and 52.26 per cent of the rural respondents are not aware about the holidays at the Fair Price Shops and thus, face problems. The respondents face problems when holidays creep in by chance. They do not get their ration supplies on the Government holidays. The responses generated with regard to this co-incidence of holidays are exhibited in Table 5.21.

Table 5.20

Responses Regarding Aware about Holidays at FPSs

S No.	Responses	Urban No.	Urban %	Rural No.	Rural %	Total No.	Total %
1.	Yes	140	50.36	100	45.04	240	48.00
2.	No	134	48.20	116	52.26	250	50.00
3.	No Response	4	1.44	6	2.70	10	2.00
	Total	278	100.00	222	100.00	500	100.00

Table 5.21
Responses Regarding Problems by Co-incidence of Holidays

S No.	*Responses*	*Urban*		*Rural*		*Total*	
		No.	*%*	*No.*	*%*	*No.*	*%*
1.	Yes	141	50.72	118	53.15	259	51.80
2.	No	129	46.40	95	42.79	224	44.80
3.	No Response	8	2.88	9	4.06	17	3.40
Total		278	100.00	222	100.00	500	100.00

Source : As per the survey conducted

Responses regarding reasons for standing in queue for a long time while drawing the ration from the FPSs are also generated from the respondents of both the sectors and have been exhibited in Table 5.22. 'Irregular shop-timings', 'more number of cards for a ration shop', 'inadequate supply', 'heavy rush etc., are the main reasons as observed during the survey which make many people wait for quite some time in long queues. Thus, the analysis indicates that the unscientific handling of the distribution results in uncertainties, long queues and hastiness which cause consumer dissatisfaction.

The respondents are also asked to narrate their experiences while purchasing goods from the PDS outlets. 262 Urban respondents and 200 rural respondents have narrated their experiences which are furnished in Table 5.23. In both the Urban and rural sectors, while further probing into the working of PDS, the following facts have also been revealed during the survey:

(a) Massive corruption at three levels in the distribution system:

(i) Officials of the Civil Supplies Department,

(ii) Dealers, and

(iii) Consumers (non-users sell sugar and other commodities in the black market).

Table 5.22
Responses Regarding Reasons for Standing in Queue for such a Long Time

Reasons / Ranks	(i) Urban No. %age	(i) Rural No. %age	(ii) Urban No. %age	(ii) Rural No. %age	(iii) Urban No. %age	(iii) Rural No. %age	(iv) Urban No. %age	(iv) Rural No. %age	(v) Urban No. %age	(v) Rural No. %age	(vi) Urban No. %age	(vi) Rural No %age
I	48	57	36	25	28	33	39	33	19	9	19	11
	19.20	28.50	14.40	12.50	11.20	16.50	15.60	16.50	7.60	4.50	7.60	5.50
II	26	53	29	23	28	39	43	29	24	19	23	11
	10.40	26.50	11.60	11.50	11.20	19.50	17.20	14.50	9.60	9.50	9.20	5.50
III	35	27	25	51	36	33	19	15	23	31	23	11
	14.00	13.50	10.00	25.50	14.40	16.50	7.60	7.50	9.20	15.50	9.20	5.50
IV	22	9	30	35	30	21	26	43	25	15	24	17
	8.80	4.50	12.00	17.50	12.00	10.50	10.40	21.50	10.00	7.50	9.60	8.50
V	21	7	26	23	24	23	18	25	36	44	25	25
	8.40	3.50	10.40	11.50	9.60	11.50	7.20	12.50	14.40	22.00	10.00	12.50
VI	20	13	18	7	27	17	15	21	23	21	29	43
	8.00	6.50	7.20	3.50	10.80	8.50	6.00	10.50	9.20	10.50	11.60	21.50
VII	15	7	24	7	22	7	18	9	20	21	30	21
	6.00	3.50	9.60	3.50	8.80	3.50	7.20	4.50	8.00	10.50	12.00	10.50
VIII	16	9	15	9	12	7	15	7	19	12	21	19
	6.40	4.50	6.00	4.50	4.80	3.50	6.00	3.50	7.60	6.00	8.40	9.50

Table 5.22 (Continued)

Ranks	Reasons (i) Urban No. %age	(i) Rural No. %age	(ii) Urban No. %age	(ii) Rural No. %age	(iii) Urban No. %age	(iii) Rural No. %age	(iv) Urban No. %age	(iv) Rural No. %age	(v) Urban No. %age	(v) Rural No. %age	(vi) Urban No. %age	(vi) Rural No %age
IX	15	7	18	11	17	7	20	3	18	11	21	13
	6.00	3.50	7.20	5.50	6.80	3.50	8.00	1.50	7.20	5.50	8.40	6.50
X	16	7	15	3	14	5	16	11	21	5	15	13
	6.40	3.50	6.00	1.50	5.60	2.50	6.40	5.50	8.40	2.50	6.00	6.50
N.R	16	4	14	6	12	8	21	4	22	12	20	16
	6.40	2.00	5.60	3.00	4.80	4.00	8.40	2.00	8.80	6.00	8.00	8.00
Total	250	200	250	200	250	200	250	200	250	200	250	200

Reasons

(i) Irregular shop timings
(ii) More number of card holders
(iii) Inadequate supply
(iv) Heavy rush
(v) Congested shops
(vi) Preference to known people
(vii) Mismanagement for release of festive quota
(viii) No Queuing system
(ix) Not opening of depots on all days of month
(x) In-Sufficiency of the depot-holder

		Urban	Rural
No. of Total Respondents	=	278	222
No Response	=	28	22
No. of Responses Generated	=	250	200

Table 5.22 (Continued)

Reasons	(vii) Urban No. %age	(vii) Rural No %age	(viii) Urban No. %age	(viii) Rural No. %age	(ix) Urban No. %age	(ix) Rural No. %age	(x) Urban No. %age	(x) Rural No. %age	Total Urban No. %age	Total Rural No. %age
I	16	9	14	9	17	5	14	9	250	200
	6.40	4.50	5.60	4.50	6.80	2.50	5.60	4.50	010.00	10.00
II	18	9	28	5	14	7	17	5	250	200
	7.20	4.50	11.20	2.50	5.60	3.50	6.80	2.50	10.00	10.00
III	24	9	23	5	19	7	17	7	250	200
	9.60	4.50	9.20	2.50	7.60	3.50	6.80	3.50	9.76	9.80
IV	21	19	24	13	19	5	20	15	241	192
	8.40	9.50	9.60	6.50	7.60	2.50	8.00	7.50	9.64	9.60
V	28	15	21	19	17	5	17	5	233	191
	11.20	7.50	8.40	9.50	6.80	2.50	6.80	2.50	9.32	9.55
VI	23	27	27	13	23	9	20	5	255	176
	9.20	13.50	10.80	6.50	9.20	4.50	8.00	2.50	9.00	8.80
VII	29	41	19	19	22	25	19	11	218	168
	11.60	20.50	7.60	9.50	8.80	12.50	7.60	5.50	8.72	8.40

Table : 5.22 (Continued)

Reasons	(vii)		(viii)		(ix)		(x)		Total	
	Urban No. %age	*Rural No %age*	*Urban No. %age*	*Rural No %age*	*Urban No. %age*	*Rural No. %age*	*Urban No. %age*	*Rural No. %age*	*Urban No. %age*	*Rural No. %qge*
VIII	20	21	36	31	26	25	27	23	207	163
	8.00	10.50	14.40	15.50	10.40	12.50	10.80	11.50	8.28	8.15
IX	21	9	23	23	40	50	22	25	215	165
	8.40	4.50	9.20	11.50	16.00	25.00	8.80	12.50	8.60	8.25
X	24	13	12	19	26	22	44	47	203	146
	9.60	6.50	4.80	9.50	10.40	11.00	17.60	23.50	8.12	7.30
N.R	26	28	23	44	27	40	33	48	214	203
	10.40	14.00	9.20	22.00	10.80	20.00	13.20	24.00	2.56	10.15
Total	250	200	250	200	250	200	250	200	2500	2000

Table 5.23

Responses Regarding Experiences while purchasing food items from the FPS

Ranks \ *Experiences*	*(i)* Urban No. %age	*(i)* Rural No. %age	*(ii)* Urban No. %age	*(ii)* Rural No. %age	*(iii)* Urban No. %age	*(iii)* Rural No. %age	*(iv)* Urban No. %age	*(iv)* Rural No. %age	*(v)* Urban No. %age	*(v)* Rural No. %age	*(vi)* Urban No. %age	*(vi)* Rural No %age
I	85	67	17	13	43	21	27	27	31	33	15	19
	32.44	33.50	6.49	6.50	16.41	10.50	10.31	13.50	11.83	16.50	5.73	9.50
II	45	27	25	39	29	25	47	23	27	23	25	27
	17.18	13.50	9.54	19.50	11.07	12.50	17.94	11.50	10.31	11.50	9.54	13.50
III	39	33	39	51	27	33	45	18	35	19	33	17
	14.89	16.50	14.89	25.50	10.31	16.50	17.18	9.00	13.36	9.50	12.60	8.50
IV	17	9	53	29	23	35	31	35	53	21	33	23
	6.49	4.50	20.23	14.50	8.78	17.50	11.83	17.50	20.23	10.50	12.60	11.50
V	19	15	27	17	53	23	39	43	37	35	33	20
	7.25	7.50	10.31	8.50	20.23	11.50	14.89	21.50	14.12	17.50	12.60	10.00
VI	17	9	34	11	39	34	29	23	29	25	37	29
	6.49	4.50	12.98	5.50	14.89	17.00	11.07	11.50	11.07	12.50	14.12	14.50

Table 5.23 (Continued)

Experiences	(i)		(ii)		(iii)		(iv)		(v)		(vi)	
Ranks	Urban No. %age	Rural No. %age	Urban No. %age	Rural No. %age	Urban No. %age	Rural No. %age	Urban No. %age	Rural No. %age	Urban No. %age	Rural No. %age	Urban No. %age	Rural No %age
VII	13 4.96	15 7.50	43 16.41	21 10.50	29 11.07	13 6.50	21 8.02	11 5.50	15 5.73	23 11.50	35 13.36	25 12.50
VIII	21 8.02	14 7.00	15 5.73	4 2.00	17 6.49	11 5.50	16 6.11	13 6.50	22 8.40	10 5.00	38 14.50	19 9.50
IX	0 0.00	0 0.00	0 0.00	0 0.00	0 0.00	0 0.00	0 0.00	2 1.00	0 0.00	0 0.00	0 0.00	0 0.00
N.R	6 2.29	11 5.50	8 3.05	15 7.50	2 0.76	5 2.50	7 2.67	5 2.50	13 4.96	11 5.50	13 4.96	21 10.50
Total	262	200	261	200	262	200	262	200	262	200	262	200

Experiences
(i) Heavy rush & long queues
(ii) Purchasing & Quarreling
(iii) Involves repeated visits
(iv) Rude behaviour of dealers
(v) Irregular supply
(vi) Black marketing & corrupt practices
(vii) Dealers' favouritism
(viii) Lumpen elements take away sugar without card
(ix) Any other

Table 5.23 (Continued)

Experiences	*(vii)* Urban No. %age	*(vii)* Rural No %age	*(viii)* Urban No. %age	*(viii)* Rural No %age	*(ix)* Urban No. %age	*(ix)* Rural No. %age	*Total* Urban No. %age	*Total* Rural No. %age
I	29	9	13	9	2	2	262	200
	11.07	4.50	4.96	4.50	0.76	1.00	11.11	11.11
II	37	23	23	11	3	2	262	200
	14.12	11.50	8.78	5.50	1.15	1.00	11.11	11.11
III	24	13	17	15	3	1	262	200
	9.16	6.50	6.49	7.50	1.15	0.50	11.11	11.11
IV	13	23	29	13	3	8	225	196
	4.96	11.50	11.07	6.50	1.15	4.00	10.81	10.89
V	27	27	15	4	5	8	255	192
	10.31	13.50	5.73	2.00	1.91	4.00	10.81	10.67
VI	46	20	22	23	1	14	254	188
	17.56	10.00	8.40	11.50	0.38	7.00	10.77	10.44

Table 5.23 (Continued)

Experiences	(vii) Urban No. %age	Rural No %age	(viii) Urban No. %age	Rural No %age	(ix) Urban No. %age	Rural No. %age	Total Urban No. %age	Rural No. %age
VII	46	34	31	23	12	19	245	184
	17.56	17.00	11.83	11.50	4.58	9.50	10.39	10.22
VIII	21	28	68	61	26	20	244	180
	8.02	14.00	25.95	30.50	9.92	10.00	10.35	10.00
IX	0	0	6	2	39	26	45	30
	0.00	0.00	2.29	1.00	14.89	13.00	1.91	1.67
N.R	19	23	38	39	168	100	274	230
	7.25	11.50	14.50	19.50	64.12	50.00	11.62	12.78
Total	262	200	262	200	262	200	2358	1800

Note :	Urban	Rural
Total No. of Respondennts	278	222
No Response	16	22
Total No. of Responses Generated	262	200

(b) PDS is not at all serving the cause of the poor and vulnerable sections of the society and on the contrary, the poor are exploited in the name of PDS.

(c) There are large number of 'bogus' ration cards in operation.

(d) About 25 per cent of the ration is sold by the dealers in the black market.

The experiences have shown that the active and meaningful public/consumer's participation is a pre-requisite for the effective and successful functioning of the PDS. The existence of effective Consumer Councils would act as a moral threat and restrict the functionaries from indulging in unhealthy practices. It is not advisable on the part of the consumers to be silent spectators when the PDS is not operating properly. Responses have also been generated with respect to the awareness about the objectives of Consumer Councils. 64.03 per cent respondents of the Urban areas and 60.36 per cent respondents of the rural areas are aware about these objectives where as 2.16 per cent respondents of the Urban sector and 2.70 per cent respondents of the rural sector have not responded in the matter as exhibited in Table 5.24.

Table 5.24
Responses Regarding Awareness about the objectives of the Consumer Councils

S No.	*Responses*	*Urban* No.	%	*Rural* No.	%	*Total* No.	%
1.	Yes	178	64.03	134	60.36	312	62.40
2.	No	94	33.81	82	36.94	176	35.20
3.	No response	6	2.16	6	2.70	12	2.40
Total		278	100.00	222	100.00	500	100.00

Source : As per the survey conducted

The Urban and the rural respondents are also of the view that the consumer councils can improve the functioning of PDS, he responses are shown in Table 5.25. Responses have also been generated with regard to the contribution of the people to consumer welfare activities. Majority of the respondents are not interested to take an active part for the establishment and working of these councils as exhibited in Table 5.26. 'Lack of time', 'nature of job', 'fear of politics and lumpen elements, 'lack of interest', 'difficulty of convincing people, etc. are considered to be important constraints which cause hurdles in the active participation of people in consumer welfare activities.

Table 5.25

Responses regarding improvement in functioning of the PDS through the Consumer Councils

S No.	*Responses*	*Urban* *No.*	*%*	*Rural* *No.*	*%*	*Total* *No.*	*%*
1.	Yes	179	64.39	122	54.96	301	60.20
2.	No	95	34.17	94	42.34	189	37.80
3.	No Response	4	1.44	6	2.70	10	2.00
Total		278	100.00	222	100.00	500	100.00

Source : As per the survey conducted

In addition to the above reasons, the respondents have also mentioned some other reasons which are categorised as under:

(a) Illiteracy of the masses,

(b) Effective participation is not possible due to lack of socio-economic awareness,

(c) Lack of co-operation from people and government officials, and

(d) Indifferent attitude of the masses.

Table 5.26
Responses Regarding Contribution to Consumer Welfare Activities

Response	*Urban*		*Rural*		*Total*	
	No.	*%*	*No.*	*%*	*No.*	*%*
Yes	121	43.52	100	45.04	221	44.20
No	151	54.32	117	52.70	268	53.60
No Response	6	2.16	5	2.26	11	2.20
Total	278	100.00	222	100.00	500	100.00

Source : As per the survey conducted

Table 5.27 shows that the respondents of both the areas have some complaints regarding the functioning of the fair price shops. 55.39 per cent respondents of the Urban areas and 52.25 per cent respondents of the rural areas have mentioned various complaints like 'FPS is not opened daily', 'working hours are inconvenient', 'heavy rush at the FPS', 'improper location', 'lack of credit facilities', etc.

During the survey , it has been revealed that the people of both the areas lodge complaints to different authorities like the ration dealer, the Food & supplies Department and the consumer councils, as exhibited in Table 5.28. There are some people who generally do not complain about the PDS. However, it is possible to identify some of the major reasons for the lack of complaints related with the PDS. First of all, some consumers have no complaints because they find the system operating to their satisfaction. Another set of consumers again do not complain because they do not know how and whom to complain.

Table 5.27
Response Regarding Complaints about Functioning of FPS

Response	*Urban*		*Rural*	
	No	*%*	*No*	*%*
Yes	154	55.39	116	52.25
No	120	43.16	101	45.50
No Response	4	1.45	5	2.25
Total	278	100.00	20	100.00

Table 5.27
If yes, the Nature of Complaints

	(i)		*(ii)*		*(iii)*		*(iv)*		*(v)*		*(vi)*		*Total*	
Ranks	*Urban No. %age*	*Rural No. %age*	*Urban No. %age*	*Rural No. %age*	*Urban No. %age*	*Rural No. %Age*	*Urban No. %age*	*Rural No. %age*	*Urban No. %age*	*Rural No. %age*	*Urban No. %age*	*Rural No. %age*	*Urban No. %age*	*Rural No. %age*
I	28	50	22	13	26	18	36	11	14	9	28	15	154	116
	18.18	43.10	14.29	11.21	16.88	15.52	23.38	9.48	9.09	7.76	18.18	12.93	16.67	16.67
II	40	31	30	21	16	14	12	16	28	14	28	20	154	116
	25.97	26.72	19.48	18.10	10.39	12.07	7.79	13.79	18.18	12.07	18.18	17.24	16.67	16.67
III	32	16	39	33	8	5	22	20	14	13	36	21	151	108
	20.78	13.79	25.32	28.45	5.19	4.31	14.29	17.24	9.09	11.21	23.38	18.10	16.34	15.52
IV	14	7	32	26	32	32	25	21	22	13	22	12	147	111
	9.09	6.03	20.78	22.41	20.78	27.59	16.23	18.10	14.29	11.21	14.29	10.34	15.91	15.95
V	22	3	12	9	30	27	27	22	34	30	22	20	147	111
	14.29	2.59	7.79	7.76	19.48	23.28	17.53	18.97	22.08	25.86	14.29	17.24	15.91	15.95
VI	11	2	12	11	40	20	31	17	34	32	14	26	142	108
	7.14	1.72	7.79	9.48	25.97	17.24	20.13	14.66	22.08	27.59	9.09	22.41	15.37	15.52
N.R	7	7	7	3	2	0	1	9	8	5	4	2	29	26
	4.55	6.03	4.55	2.59	1.30	0.00	0.65	7.76	5.19	4.31	2.60	1.72	3.14	3.74
Total	154	116	154	116	154	116	154	116	154	116	154	116	924	696

Nature of Complaints

(i) FPS is not Opened Daily. *(ii)* Inconvenient Hours *(iii)* Heavy Rush *(iv)* Improper Location. *(v)* Inadequate & Irregular Supply. *(vi)* Lack of Credit Facility.

Source : As per the Survey Conducted

Table 5.28
Responses Regarding Lodging Complaints to different authrorities

Response	*Urban*		*Rural*		*Total*	
	No	*%*	*No.*	*%*	*No.*	*%*
(i) To the R.D	102	36.69	92	41.44	194	38.80
(ii) F & S Deptt.	89	32.02	85	38.28	174	34.80
(iii) CPDRD	62	22.30	30	13.52	92	18.40
(iv) No response	25	8.99	15	6.76	40	8.00
Total	278	100.00	222	100.00	500	100.00

Source : As per the survey conducted.

About the future of PDS, quite a large number of the respondents both from the Urban and the rural areas, are of the opinion that PDS would not be a success. This indicates that ideologically they are with the PDS, but they are disappointed at its performance which shows the low credibility of the PDS.

The respondents are also asked whether they would like to suggest any changes in the format and the procedure for issuing of the ration card. 59.71 per cent respondents of the Urban areas and 54.05 per cent respondents of the rural areas have given some suggestions with regard to improving the procedure for issuing of the ration card, as exhibited in Table 5.29. Most of the respondents are of the view that the ration card should be in a booklet or bank pass-book form with good quality paper.

261 respondents of the Urban areas and 205 from the rural areas have also suggested some measures to avoid delay and quick disposal of the customers at the FPSs. First rank has been given by the majority of the people to the suggestion 'The number of FPSs should be increased'. Responses have also been generated with regard to the other suggestions given by the respondents of both the areas as formulated in Table 5.30.

Table 5.29

Responses Regarding any suggestions to improve the procedure of issuing ration card

Response	*Urban* No	*Urban* %age	*Rural* No	*Rural* %age
Yes	166	59.71	120	54.05
No	111	39.93	99	44.60
N.R.	1	0.36	3	1.35
Total	278	100.00	222	100.00

If Yes, the Suggestions

Rank	*(i) FPS Dealers should be Authorised*				*(ii) Issue of Ration Card should be Simultaneous*				*(iii) Time Limit should be Fixed*				*Total*			
	Urban		*Rural*		*Urban*		*Rural*		*Urban*		*Rural*		*Urban*		*Rural*	
	No.	*%age*	*No.*	*%age*	*No.*	*%age*	*No.*	*%age*	*No.*	*%age*	*No.*	*%age*	*No.*	*%age*	*No.*	*%age*
I	54	32.53	53	44.17	58	34.94	32	26.67	54	32.53	35	29.17	166	33.33	120	33.33
II	54	32.53	34	28.33	58	34.94	41	34.17	52	31.33	45	37.50	164	32.93	120	33.33
III	55	33.13	30	25.00	46	27.71	47	39.17	54	32.53	33	27.50	155	31.12	110	30.56
N.R.	3	1.81	3	2.50	4	2.41	0	0.00	6	3.61	7	5.83	13	2.61	10	2.78
Total	166	100.00	120	100.00	166	100.00	120	100.00	166	100.00	120	100.00	498	100.00	360	100.00

Source : As per the survey conducted

Table 5.30

Responses Regarding Suggestions to Avoid Delay and Quick Disposal of Customers at the FPS

Suggestions	*(i)*		*(ii)*		*(iii)*		*(iv)*		*(v)*		*(vi)*	
Ranks	*Urban* No. *%age*	*Rural* No. *%age*	*Urban* No. *%age*	*Rural* No. *%age*	*Urban* No. *%age*	*Rural* No. *%age*	*Urban* No. *%age*	*Rural* No. *%age*	*Urban* No. *%age*	*Rural* No. *%age*	*Urban* No. *%age*	*Rural* No *%age*
I	93	75	27	19	24	16	39	22	26	20	21	22
	35.63	36.59	10.34	9.27	9.20	7.80	14.94	10.73	9.96	9.76	8.05	10.73
II	43	35	49	37	35	29	14	13	23	14	27	21
	16.48	17.07	18.77	18.05	13.41	14.15	5.36	6.34	8.81	6.83	10.34	10.24
III	41	33	39	41	45	37	27	23	22	14	32	18
	15.71	16.10	14.94	20.00	17.24	18.05	10.34	11.22	8.43	6.83	12.26	8.78
IV	11	11	47	28	31	25	33	37	25	18	43	34
	4.21	5.37	18.01	13.66	11.88	12.20	12.64	18.05	9.58	8.78	16.48	16.59
V	21	15	43	19	39	25	33	26	47	34	17	22
	8.05	7.32	16.48	9.27	14.94	12.20	12.64	12.68	18.01	16.59	6.51	10.73
VI	19	11	25	19	53	39	41	24	24	32	36	24
	7.28	5.37	9.58	9.27	20.31	19.02	15.71	11.71	9.20	15.61	13.79	11.71
VII	11	11	25	17	17	18	21	18	33	27	20	21
	4.21	5.37	9.58	8.29	6.51	8.78	8.05	8.78	12.64	13.17	7.66	10.24

Table 5.30 (Continued)
Responses Regarding Suggestions to Avoid Delay and Quick Disposal of Customers at the FPS

Suggestions	(i)		(ii)		(iii)		(iv)		(v)		(vi)	
Ranks	*Urban* No. %age	*Rural* No. %age	*Urban* No. %age	*Rural* No. %age	*Urban* No. %age	*Rural* No. %age	*Urban* No. %age	*Rural* No. %age	*Urban* No. %age	*Rural* No. %age	*Urban* No. %age	*Rural* No %age
VIII	5	3	3	10	7	4	28	27	25	20	30	20
	1.92	1.46	1.15	4.88	2.68	1.95	10.73	13.17	9.58	9.76	11.49	9.76
IX	13	3	2	6	4	2	12	8	12	11	13	7
	4.98	1.46	0.77	2.93	1.53	0.98	4.60	3.90	4.60	5.37	4.98	3.41
X	3	1	0	3	3	5	5	5	19	9	15	11
	1.15	0.49	0.00	1.46	1.15	2.44	1.92	2.44	7.28	4.39	5.75	5.37
N.R	1	7	1	6	3	5	8	2	5	6	7	5
	0.38	3.41	0.38	2.93	1.15	2.44	3.07	0.98	1.92	2.93	2.68	2.44
Total	261	205	261	205	261	205	261	205	261	205	261	205

Suggestions

(i) Increase in No. of FPS *(ii)* Number of Card Holders should not increase *(iii)* Regular Supply from the Central Pool *(iv)* Separate Dates for each block within a municipal ward *(v)* Appointment of Experienced staff *(vi)* Goods should be pre-weighed & pre packed *(vii)* Shops should be kept open on holidays *(viii)* Festival quotas should be released well in advance. *(ix)* Separate doors for enterence & exit. *(x)* Special counters for women.

Table 5.30 (Continued)

Suggestions	(vii)		(viii)		(ix)		(x)		Total	
Ranks	*Urban* No. %age	*Rural* No. %age	*Urban* No. %age	*Rural* No. %age	*Urban* No. %age	*Rural* No. %age	*Urban* No. %age	*Rural* No. %age	*Urban* No. %age	*Rural* No. %age
I	17	13	9	8	5	4	0	6	261	205
	6.51	6.34	3.45	3.90	1.92	1.95	0.00	2.93	10.00	10.00
II	29	17	23	18	9	10	9	11	261	205
	11.11	8.29	8.81	8.78	3.45	4.88	3.45	5.37	10.00	10.00
III	21	22	12	5	13	8	9	4	261	205
	8.05	10.73	4.60	2.44	4.98	3.90	3.45	1.95	10.00	10.00
IV	21	22	28	20	17	7	5	3	261	205
	8.05	10.73	10.73	9.76	6.51	3.41	1.92	1.46	10.00	10.00
V	21	18	24	19	7	7	9	10	261	195
	8.05	8.78	9.20	9.27	2.68	3.41	3.45	4.88	10.00	9.51
VI	17	12	24	27	3	8	19	6	261	202
	6.51	5.85	9.20	13.17	1.15	3.90	7.28	2.93	10.00	9.85
VII	45	32	20	15	32	25	29	16	253	199
	17.24	15.61	7.66	7.32	12.26	12.20	11.11	7.80	9.69	9.71

Table 5.30 (Continued.)

Ranks	Suggestions (vii) Urban No. %age	(vii) Rural No. %age	(viii) Urban No. %age	(viii) Rural No. %age	(ix) Urban No. %age	(ix) Rural No. %age	(x) Urban No. %age	(x) Rural No. %age	Total Urban No. %age	Total Rural No. %age
VIII	35	30	51	43	43	32	31	16	258	205
	13.41	14.63	19.54	20.98	16.48	15.61	11.88	7.80	9.89	10.00
IX	39	26	29	18	74	58	68	49	266	188
	14.94	12.68	11.11	8.78	28.35	28.29	26.05	23.90	10.19	9.17
X	15	10	41	27	57	43	79	71	237	185
	5.75	4.88	15.71	13.17	21.84	20.98	30.27	34.63	9.08	9.02
N.R	1	3	0	5	1	3	3	13	30	56
	0.38	1.46	0.00	2.44	0.38	1.46	1.15	6.34	1.15	2.73
Total	261	205	261	205	261	205	261	205	2610	2050

Note	Urban	Rural
Total No. of Respondents	278	222
No Response	17	17
No. of Respones Generated	261	205

Table 5.31

Responses Regarding Suggestions to Improve the Overall Functioning of the PDS

	(i) The Quality of All the Items & Quantity of sugar should be enhanced				*(ii) Exclusion of High Salaried Urban Professionals*				*(iii) Fixing of Income Limits*				*(iv) Sufficient Arrangements for Transportation & Ware-Housing*				*Total*			
	Urban		*Rural*		*Urban*		*Rural*		*Urban*		*Rural*		*Urban*		*Rural*		*Urban*		*Rural*	
Ranks	*No*	*%age*	*No*	*%age*	*No*	*%age*	*No*	*%age*	*No*	*%age*	*No*	*%age*	*No*	*%age*	*No*	*%age*	*No*	*%age*	*No*	*%age*
I	110	41.51	79	38.16	61	23.02	38	18.36	46	17.36	44	21.26	48	18.11	46	22.22	265	25	207	25
II	77	29.06	35	16.91	60	22.64	48	23.18	62	23.4	52	25.12	66	24.91	72	34.78	265	25	207	25
III	44	16.6	37	17.87	68	25.66	78	37.68	90	33.96	69	33.33	50	18.87	22	10.63	252	23.77	206	24.88
IV	34	12.83	56	27.06	76	28.68	41	19.81	60	22.64	39	18.84	65	24.53	50	24.16	235	22.17	186	22.46
N.R.	0	0	0	0	0	0	2	0.97	7	2.64	3	1.45	36	13.58	17	8.21	43	4.06	22	2.66
Total	265	100	207	100	265	100	207	100	265	100	207	100	265	100	207	100	1060	100	828	100

	Urban	Rural
Total No. of Responses	278	229
No Response	13	15
Total No. of Responses Generated	265	204

Source : As per the Survey Conducted.

The respondents have also suggested some other measures as to how PDS could be improved and become a useful programme for them. Table 5.31 shows the responses of the respondents of both the areas, regarding suggestions with regard to improving the overall functioning of the PDS.

In view of the above experiences so far, it has become useful to answer some other questions regarding the role which the PDS may be able to play in the coming years. This is related to the objectives which the PDS, as a part of the food supply system, can hope to serve. There is little doubt that the PDS is an availability and price intervention system rather than the one which increases or maintains the availability of income earning opportunities. This system can, therefore, contribute to the protection of the consumption of its users against increases in the open market prices. After all, the PDS is expected to make available, at pre-determined, relatively stable prices, specified amounts' of specified commodities to its intended beneficiaries. Thus, the primary objective of the PDS has to be the protection of the consumption levels of the relatively poorer population with sticky incomes and irregular and inadequate or ineffective employment.

Chapter–6
Problems, Conclusion and Suggestions

Problems

The Public Distribution System in Jammu Region as of today might have attained a degree of success in the periphery of Jammu City, otherwise the whole system has collapsed and is no longer an attractive distribution system for either the consumers or the people running the ration shops. Most of the high income group individuals have probably never seen the interior of a ration shop. The middle income group too rarely makes use of this facility. It is now only those belonging to lower income groups who make use of these outlets regularly. The persons running these outlets do not seem to be interested in this business and the people also complain that some of these shops remain closed for days together and never display the price lists. Although the listed price for the sale of sugar is Rs. 9.05 per kg., none of the outlets is selling it for less than Rs. 9.50 per kg.

The officials of the agencies engaged in the whole distribution system have admitted that the present system has outlived its utility in Jammu region. But still there are numerous problems which cause hurdles in the effective and proper functioning of the PDS operations. During the survey, the responses have also been generated with regard to other problems faced by the agencies as exhibited in Tables 6.1, 6.2 and 6.3.

Table 6.1

Responses of the Agencies Regarding Main Bottlenecks in the Conduct of Procurement Operations

Bottlenecks

Ranks	Urban No. %age	Rural No. %age	Urban No. %age	Rural No. %age	Urban No. %age	Rural No. %age	Urban No. %age	Rural No. %age	Urban No. %age	Rural No. %age	Urban No. %age	Rural No. %age	Urban No. %age	Rural No. %age	Total Urban No. %age	Total Rural No. %age
I	11	8	7	6	6	3	5	3	1	0	0	0	0	0	30	20
	36.67	40.00	23.33	30.00	20.00	15.00	16.67	15.00	3.33	0.00	0.00	0.00	0.00	0.00	14.29	14.29
II	8	6	12	9	5	2	3	1	2	2	0	0	0	0	30	20
	26.67	30.00	40.00	45.00	16.67	10.00	10.00	5.00	6.67	10.00	0.00	0.00	0.00	0.00	14.29	14.29
III	9	6	5	5	9	8	6	1	1	0	0	0	0	0	30	20
	30.00	30.00	16.67	25.00	30.00	40.00	20.00	5.00	3.33	0.00	0.00	0.00	0.00	0.00	14.29	14.29
IV	2	0	3	0	10	5	12	10	3	3	0	0	0	0	30	18
	6.67	0.00	10.00	0.00	33.33	25.00	40.00	50.00	10.00	15.00	0.00	0.00	0.00	0.00	14.29	12.86
V	0	0	3	0	0	2	2	3	15	8	0	0	0	0	20	13
	0.00	0.00	10.00	0.00	0.00	10.00	6.67	15.00	50.00	40.00	0.00	0.00	0.00	0.00	9.52	9.29
VI	0	0	0	0	0	0	2	2	1	2	15	7	0	0	18	11
	0.00	0.00	0.00	0.00	0.00	0.00	6.67	10.00	3.33	10.00	50.00	35.00	0.00	0.00	8.57	7.89
VII	0	0	0	0	0	0	0	0	0	0	10	3	10	5	20	8
	0.00	0.00	0.00	0.00	0.00	0.00	0.00	0.00	0.00	0.00	33.33	15.00	3.33	25.0	9.52	5.71

Table 6.1 (Continued)

Ranks															*Total*	
	Urban No. %age	*Rural* No. %age	*Urban* No. %age	*Rural* No. %age	*Urban* No. %age	*Rural* No. %age	*Urban* No. %age	*Rural* No. %age	*Urban* No. %age	*Rural* No. %age	*Urban* No. %age	*Rural* No. %age	*Urban* No. %age	*Rural* No. %age	*Urban* No. %age	*Rural* No. %age
N.R.	0 0.00	0 0.00	0 0.00	0 0.00	0 0.00	0 0.00	0 0.00	0 0.00	7 23.33	8 25.00	8 16.67	10 50.00	20 66.67	15 75.00	32 15.24	30 21.43
Total	30	20	30	20	30	20	30	20	30	20	30	20	30	20	210	140

Bottlenecks

(i) Inadequate Staff

(ii) Lack of adequate Transport Facilities

(iii) Lack of Coordination

(iv) Corruption Among Staff

(v) Unfair Practices

(vi) Red Tapism in FCI's District Office

(vii) Any Other

Source : As per the Survey Conducted

Table 6.2

Responses of the Agencies Regarding reasons for Storage Losses

Reasons

Ranks	(i) *Infestation due to Long Time Storage* *Urban* *No*	*%age*	*Rural* *No*	*%age*	(ii) *Damagae from Rats, Birds etc.* *Urban* *No*	*%age*	*Rural* *No*	*%age*	(iii) *No Improvement in Storage Facilities* *Urban* *No*	*%age*	*Rural* *No*	*%age*
I	11	36.67	8	40.00	6	20.00	5	25.00	9	30.00	7	35.00
II	7	23.33	3	15.00	6	20.00	8	40.00	8	26.67	8	40.00
III	8	26.67	5	25.00	10	33.33	6	30.00	5	16.67	5	25.00
IV	3	10.00	3	15.00	8	26.67	0	0.00	8	26.67	0	0.00
N.R	1	3.33	1	5.00	0	0.00	1	5.00	0	0.00	0	0.00
Total	30	100.00	20	100.00	30	100.00	20	100.00	30	100.00	20	100.00

Ranks	(iv) Pilferage & Improper Handling Urban No	%age	Rural No	%age	Total Urban No	%age	Rural No	%age
I	4	13.33	0	0.00	30	25.00	20	25.00
II	9	30.00	1	5.00	30	25.00	20	25.00
III	7	23.33	2	10.00	30	25.00	18	22.50
IV	8	26.67	7	35.00	27	22.50	10	12.50
N.R	2	6.67	10	50.00	3	2.50	12	15.00
Total	30	100.00	20	100.00	120	100.00	80	100.00

Source: As per the survey conducted

Table 6.3
Responses of the Agencies Regarding Defects in the Present Public Distribution System

Defects

Ranks	(i)		(ii)		(iii)		(iv)		(v)		(vi)		(vii)		Total	
	Urban No. %age	Rural No. %age	Urban No. %age	Rural No. %age	Urban No. %age	Rural No. %age	Urban No. %age	Rural No. %age	Urban No. %age	Rural No. %age	Urban No. %age	Rural No. %age	Urban No. %age	Rural No. %age	Urban No. %age	Rural No. %age
I	12	9	8	5	6	5	4	1	0	0	0	0	0	0	30	20
	40.00	45.00	26.67	25.00	20.00	25.00	13.33	5.00	0.00	0.00	0.00	0.00	0.00	0.00	14.29	14.29
II	8	6	10	8	6	3	3	2	3	1	0	0	0	0	30	20
	26.67	30.00	33.33	40.00	20.00	15.00	10.00	10.00	10.00	5.00	0.00	0.00	0.00	0.00	14.29	14.29
III	6	3	7	6	10	9	5	0	2	2	0	0	0	0	30	20
	20.00	15.00	23.33	30.00	33.33	45.00	16.67	0.00	6.67	10.00	0.00	0.00	0.00	0.00	14.29	14.29
IV	4	2	5	0	8	2	10	9	3	7	0	0	0	0	30	20
	13.33	10.00	16.67	0.00	26.67	10.00	33.33	45.00	10.00	35.00	0.00	0.00	0.00	0.00	14.29	14.29
V	0	0	0	1	0	1	7	5	7	10	0	0	0	0	14	17
	0.00	0.00	0.00	5.00	0.00	5.00	23.33	25.00	23.33	50.00	0.00	0.00	0.00	0.00	6.67	12.14
VI	0	0	0	0	0	0	1	0	5	0	0	0	0	0	6	0
	0.00	0.00	0.00	0.00	0.00	0.00	3.33	0.00	16.67	0.00	0.00	0.00	0.00	0.00	2.86	0.00
VII	0	0	0	0	0	0	0	0	2	0	0	0	0	0	2	0
	0.00	0.00	0.00	0.00	0.00	0.00	0.00	0.00	6.67	0.00	0.00	0.00	0.00	0.00	0.95	0.00

Ranks	(i)		(ii)		(iii)		(iv)		(v)		(vi)		(viii)		Total	
	Urban No. %age	Rural No. %age	Urban No. %age	Rural No. %age	Urban No. %age	Rural No. %age	Urban No. %age	Rural No. %age	Urban No. %age	Rural No. %age	Urban No. %age	Rural No. %age	Urban No. %age	Rural No. %age	Urban No. %age	Rural No. %age
N.R.	0	0	0	0	0	0	0	3	8	0	30	20	30	20	68	43
	0.00	0.00	0.00	0.00	0.00	0.00	0.00	15.00	26.67	0.00	100.00	100.00	100.00	100.00	32.38	30.71
Total	30	20	30	20	30	20	30	20	30	20	30	20	30	20	210	140

Defects

(i) PDS is not a success

(ii) Scope for black marketing

(iii) Policy is not practicable

(iv) Lack of political will

(v) Corruption

(vi) Irregular supply

(vii) No proper supply

(a) Main Bottlenecks in the conduct of procurement operations.

Bottlenecks in order of ranking are:

(i) Inadequate staff;

(ii) Lack of adequate transport facilities;

(iii) Lack of co-ordination; and

(iv) Corruption and other unfair practices.

(b) Reasons for storage Losses

Reasons in order of ranking are:

(i) Infestation due to long-time storage;

(ii) No improvement in storage facilities;

(iii) Damage from the rats, birds, etc; and

(iv) Pilferage and improper handling.

(c) Defects in the present PDS

Defects in order of ranking are:

(i) PDS is not a success;

(ii) Scope for black marketing;

(iii) Impracticable policy;

(iv) and others.

Besides many other problems, there are other complaints also for which the responses have been generated from the dealers dealing in the distribution system regarding customers' complaints, satisfaction with the present PDS, etc.

Out of the total dealers contacted during the survey, 66.10 per cent of the urban areas and 58.54 per cent of the rural areas, have opined that the customers have complained about the poor quality, insufficient quota, under weighment of the items, heavy rush and misbehaviour with the ladies. The per centages given in Table 6.4 are self-explanatory.

It has also been revealed during the survey that 49.15 per cent of the urban dealers and 63.42 per cent of the rural dealers are not satisfied with this present system of distribution due to various problems. Table 6.5 shows the responses with regard to the problems.

Operationally, the study has revealed that from the stage of the management of ration cards to the stage of actual issuing of the ration, the PDS suffers from many short comings.

The claim, that the PDS provides support to the farmers, is also not true. Hardly any coarse grain is ever purchased from the farmers. For building up its rice-stocks, the PDS mostly depends on the levies from the rice mills. Even for the wheat purchases, there is a growing dependence on the middle men. Infact, the support to farmers has transferred into support to rice millers and other middle men. In any case, the minimum support prices have taken every factor into consideration except the level of prices, which the farmers have to pay for their own requirements.

Problems in Targeting the PDS

The reforms programme is likely to have an adverse impact on the poor in the short run maintaining or improving the welfare of the poor requires either increasing or targeting the present untargeted safety nets. Though, at present, the extent of benefits derived by the poor from the PDS is low, there are several practical problems in targeting.

The main concentration of the PDS operations is in the urban areas. It is because the unit cost of serving high density population with better infrastructural facilities in terms of transport and storage network, etc. is lower in comparison to serving scattered clusters of population separated by long distances and connected by poor roads.

However, there are practical difficulties in implementing such suggestions as demonstrated by the experience of other subsidy-linked programmes such as the Integrated Rural Development Programme (IRDP).

Table 6.4

Responses Regarding Receiving Customer Complaints

Response	*Urban* No.	*Urban* %	*Rural* No.	*Rural* %
Yes	78	66.10	48	58.54
No	40	33.90	34	41.46
Total	118	100.00	82	100.00

If yes, the Nature of complaints

Ranks	*Urban No. %age*	*Rural No. %age*	*Urban No. %age*	*Rural No. %age*	*Urban No. %age*	*Rural No. %age*	*Urban No. %age*	*Rural No. %age*	*Urban No. %age*	*Rural No. %age*	*Urban No. %age*	*Rural No. %age*	*Urban No. %age*	*Rural No. %age*	*Total Urban No. %age*	*Total Rural No. %age*
I	42	20	20	16	6	6	6	2	0	0	2	4	2	0	78	48
	53.85	41.67	25.64	33.33	7.69	12.50	7.69	4.17	0.00	0.00	2.56	8.33	2.56	0.00	14.29	14.29
II	16	14	16	0	8	4	2	20	8	6	4	0	4	4	78	48
	20.51	29.17	20.51	0.00	10.26	8.33	2.56	41.67	10.26	12.50	5.13	0.00	5.13	8.33	14.29	14.29
III	10	14	20	22	26	4	6	4	12	4	4	0	0	0	78	48
	12.82	29.17	25.64	45.83	33.33	8.33	7.69	8.33	15.38	8.33	5.13	0.00	0.00	0.00	14.29	14.29
IV	10	0	8	8	16	12	22	6	10	14	2	0	2	0	70	40
	12.82	0.00	10.26	16.67	20.51	25.0	28.21	12.50	12.82	29.17	2.56	0.00	2.56	0.00	12.82	11.90

Ranks															TOTAL	
	Urban No. %age	*Rural* No. %age	*Urban* No. %age	*Rural* No. %age	*Urban* No. %age	*Rural* No. %age	*Urban* No. %age	*Rural* No. %age	*Urban* No. %age	*Rural* No. %age	*Urban* No. %age	*Rural* No. %age	*Urban* No. %age	*Rural* No. %age	*Urban* No. %age	*Rural* No. %age
V	0	0	6	0	14	16	6	8	12	8	16	4	2	0	56	36
	0.00	0.00	7.69	0.00	17.95	33.33	7.69	16.67	15.38	16.67	20.51	8.33	2.56	0.00	10.26	10.71
VI	0	0	8	2	8	4	4	0	14	4	22	10	0	0	56	20
	0.00	0.00	10.26	4.17	10.26	8.33	5.13	0.00	17.95	8.33	28.21	20.83	0.00	0.00	10.26	5.95
VII	0	0	0	0	0	0	0	0	0	0	6	2	24	2	30	4
	0.00	0.00	0.00	0.00	0.00	0.00	0.00	0.00	0.00	0.00	7.69	4.17	30.77	4.17	5.49	1.19
N.R.	0	0	0	0	0	2	12	8	22	12	22	28	44	42	100	92
	0.00	0.00	0.00	0.00	0.00	4.17	15.38	16.67	28.21	25.00	28.21	58.33	56.41	87.50	18.32	27.38
Total	78	48	78	48	78	48	58	48	78	48	78	48	78	48	546	336

Nature of Complaints

(i) Poor Quality
(ii) Insufficient Quota
(iii) Non-availability
(iv) Under Weighing
(v) Heavy rush
(vi) Misbehaviour with Ladies
(vii) Not opening on all days

Source: As per the survey conducted.

Table : 6.5
Responses Regarding Satisfaction with Present System of Distribution

Response	*Urban*		*Rural*	
	No.	%	*No.*	%
Yes	60	50.85	30	36.58
No	58	49.15	52	63.42
Total	118	100.00	82	100.00

If No, What are the Problems?

															Total	
	Urban	*Rural*	*Urban*	*Rural*	*Urban*	*Rural*	*Urban*	*Rural*	*Urban*	*Rural*	*Urban*	*Rural*	*Urban*	*Rural*	*Urban*	*Rural*
	No.	*No.*	*No.*	*No.*	*No.*	*No.*	*No.*	*No.*	*No.*	*No.*	*No.*	*No.*	*No.*	*No.*	*No.*	*No.*
Ranks	*%age*	*%age*	*%age*	*%age*	*%age*	*%age*	*%age*	*%age*	*%age*	*%age*	*%age*	*%age*	*%age*	*%age*	*%age*	*%age*
I	24	12	8	20	18	16	4	0	2	0	2	4	58	52		
	41.38	23.08	13.79	38.46	31.03	30.77	6.90	0.00	3.45	0.00	3.45	7.69	16.67	16.67		
II	20	10	16	10	2	6	12	16	6	8	2	2	58	52		
	34.48	19.23	27.59	19.23	3.45	11.54	20.69	30.77	10.34	15.38	3.45	16.67	16.67	16.67		
III	8	16	16	8	26	18	2	4	6	4	0	2	58	52		
	13.79	30.77	27.59	15.38	44.83	34.62	3.45	7.69	10.34	7.69	0.00	3.85	16.67	16.67		

Ranks	Urban	Rural	Urban	Rural	Urban	Rural	Urban	Rural	Urban	Rural	Urban	Rural	Total Urban	Total Rural
	No.	No.	No.	No.	No.	No.	No.	No.	No.	No.	No.	No.	No.	No.
	%age	%age	%age	%age	%age	%age	%age	%age	%age	%age	%age	%age	%age	%age
IV	2	4	6	6	8	6	16	14	8	4	2	4	42	38
	3.45	7.69	10.34	11.54	13.79	11.54	27.59	26.92	13.79	7.69	3.45	7.69	12.07	12.18
V	4	2	6	6	2	0	6	2	10	2	6	2	34	14
	6.90	3.85	10.34	11.54	3.45	0.00	10.34	3.85	3.45	0.00	20.69	3.85	6.32	3.85
N.R.	0	4	4	0	0	4	14	14	24	34	34	36	76	92
	0.00	7.69	6.90	0.00	0.00	7.69	24.14	26.92	41.38	65.38	58.62	69.23	21.84	29.49
Total	58	52	58	52	58	52	58	52	58	52	58	52	348	312

Problems

(i) Supply of low quality

(ii) Location is not Good

(iii) Commission on sales is less

(iv) Improper Timings

(v) Less No. of FPS

(vi) Behaviour is Irritating

Source: As per the survey conducted

Conclusion:

India's Public Distribution System (PDS) may be a much-maligned institution but it has some points to its credit. It routinely performs remarkable feats like ensuring the reaching of essential food grains to highly inaccessible regions. Arguably, it is the largest single retail system in the world in terms of the population it serves.

The Five Year Plan documents have repeatedly stressed that the PDS is a deliberate social policy instrument and forms part of the permanent strategy of the Government to ensure adequate availability of food grains for such poor households who come forward and take advantage of the system. Revamping the PDS is another structural programme. In our country, the present regime has been emphasizing quite stridently its commitment to strengthen the PDS. This is undoubtedly a very useful strategy and may lighten the burden of adjustment for the weaker sections. This is also in keeping with the basic thrust of the PDS which is a complementary element of the food economy which attempts to supply essential goods to the poorer sections at stable and affordable prices, particularly in view of the persistent inflationary pressures.

Based on the review of some studies, the present study is an addition to the current literature on the subject as it endeveours to study the major objectives of the PDS i.e. adequacy of the rural coverage; management of the fair price shops under the scheme, consumers perception and the image of the PDS at work, administrative and the managerial aspects of the PDS at the Central and the State level to assess the ability to run this system effectively and to suggest suitable measures in the light of the problems identified. Thus the present study proposes to examine the major objectives of the PDS and their actual impact. In other words, the study seeks to examine the gap between the promise and performance of the PDS.

The shortcomings noticed in the functioning of PDS as it is structured presently, range from, it being urban-biased and pro-rich to its ineffectiveness in reaching the poor. The system has, however, come to stay, not withstanding its shortcomings, because millions of India's poor derive direct or indirect benefits from the very existence of this system. The World Bank in their report of 1991 has observed that "poverty consideration will compel India to sustain publicly sponsored foodgrain procurement, storage and distribution efforts. These programmes are even more important in a period of economic down turn and adjustment, to ensure an adequate safety-net".

Effectiveness of the PDS and its capacity to serve the vulnerable sections depend, in addition to the macro aspects connected with the national food policy, on a large number of policy decisions regarding the operational and organisational aspects of the PDS. These issues are largely a matter of decision making by the state governments. In the present study, an attempt has been made to analyze the organisation and the management of PDS in Jammu Region. Management structure of the PDS at the national level includes policy formulation, fixing of objectives, strategy for procurement and distribution of foodgrains and other essential commodities. In order to operate the PDS effectively, the Central Government also issues guidelines to the states from time to time regarding the operational details of the PDS. In the states, it is the Food and Civil Supplies Department which looks after the PDS. The major decisions in the organisational & administrative set up of the PDS are the issue of ration card, commodity coverage, the ration scales, the periodicity of purchases, the PDS's issue prices and the quality of its supplies.

Maintaining or improving the welfare of the poor, requires either increasing or targeting the present untargeted safety nets through subsidising poor households, dual price system, food for work, identifying target families for PDS, quantity to be distributed and subsidy to be provided for targeted PDS.

Thus, the analysis has indicated that the organisational and the managerial structure from the central level down to the district level is weak and lacks unity of purpose. The overall perception of the PDS of both the urban and the rural respondents is not the same. There is a slight difference between the responses of the respondents of both the areas.

Apart from some very important general factors affecting FPS operations such as adequacy of central allocations and the extent of coverage, there are some specific factors that need to be analyzed. This set of factors is related to the administrative arrangements made for public distribution and which directly affects the operations and viability of the licensed retail outlets. Some of the important variables that directly affect the administrative arrangements are the number of cards or ration units attached to each retail outlet, number of FPSs and their size, various aspects of choice of FPS licencee, arrangements for supplying stocks of PDS commodities to FPSs, the profit margins allowed to the FPSs dealers and some other miscellaneous factors.

The inferences, that have been drawn on various issues by analyzing the information collected from the FPS dealers have exhibited that a two-tier system of FPSs prevalent in the state. But in Jammu Region, both in the urban and rural areas, the largest single group of FPSs are run by private people who are authorised by the State Civil Supplies Deptt. to supply the PDS commodities at the fixed prices to the card holders according to the fixed entitlements. The main objective of the FPS dealer in running this business, as revealed during the survey is 'Profit'. But at the same time, majority of the dealers are not satisfied with the profit margins allowed to them by the Government Some dealers are of the view that corruption at the supervisory staff level compels them to indulge in blackmarketing and other malpractices and creates hurdles in providing better services to their customers. It has also been observed during the survey that in both the urban and the rural areas of Jammu Region, the sale of rationed and non-rationed commodities from the same retail point is allowed in order to improve the viability of FPS. Thus, it has been observed that the rules, procedures, policies and administrative arrangements which determine the viability and effectiveness of FPS as a means of serving the consumers and giving them fair and reasonable access to the PDS goods have not been consciously recognised and examined.

An attempt has also been made to examine the operational work of the PDS from the point of view of the consumers. The major focus of the analysis has been first, on the consumers' attitude towards the PDS as such and second, on the procedural difficulties in the actual operation of the system. The findings have shown that an overwhelming majority of the respondents from the urban areas and slightly more than half of the respondents from the rural areas are aware about the objectives of the PDS. The respondents have also shown their preference for the food items distributed under the present system of public distribution inspite of various drawbacks in it. This is because, in times of scarcities and shortages, this is the only system which provides them, essential commodities at the fair prices. While further probing into the working of PDS, responses have also been generated with regard to the experiences gained by different customers while visiting and purchasing the ration items from their respective fair price shops in both the sectors. Thus, the findings have revealed that an active and meaningful public participation is a pre-requisite for the effective and successful functioning of the PDS.

All these observations lead to give an indication that the hypotheses, based on the premise that the management of public distribution system in Jammu Region is not in accordance with the modern principles, functions, Policies and procedures of management, are correct.

The study comprises the following six chapters:

I Introductory and Research Methodology;

II Review of Literature;

III The Administration and the Organisation of the PDS;

IV Operational Aspects of the Fair Price Shops;

V The Consumer and the PDS; and

VI Problems, Conclusion and Suggestions.

Suggestions

The dangers of increasing poverty and rising prices which are constantly present in the economy can not be effectively dealt with without strengthening the PDS. The most important recommendation made in this presentation is the need to target the PDS to the poor. PDS in its present universal form serves the poor only marginally, but consumes a subsidy of more than Rs. 5,000 crore. There have been some tentative steps taken by a few State Governments towards targeting PDS to the poor. The first step, therefore, is to change the direction of public distribution, the flow in the reformed system running in the direction of the targeted rural and urban poor who will clearly know exactly what their rights are in the supply system. There is thus an urgent need to introduce special measures for radically improving the level of access to essential commodities especially for the poor.

In the present circumstances, it is both necessary and desirable to introduce a certain kind of target-group orientation in the PDS. This is essential in order to grant improved access to the PDS supplies for those who become worse-off through a process of rising prices as well as to improve the overall price-restraining influence of the PDS. There are suggestions to eliminate income-tax payers, owners of motor vehicles and telephones, those employed in the organised sector etc. In rural areas, criteria such as land holding and live stock can be used to remove non-poor from the PDS.

The three-member committee of the ministers set up by the Centre to advise the Government on evolving a national policy on the PDS, has suggested the following measures:

(a) It is imperative that atleast 20 kgs. of food grains should be made available to each family per month.

(b) There should be exclusion of better off sections of population from access to PDS. Such as:

- Income-tax assesses;
- Professionals like Doctors, Lawyers, CA's, Architects;
- All those registered under Shops and Establishment Act.
- Employees of Government, Public Sector and Private Sector.
- All IRDP beneficiaries, except Landless Labourers, Rural Artisans, Small/Marginal Farmers.

(c) Quantity of foodgrains and other commodities being issued to States and Union Territories should not be reduced.

(d) Steps should be taken to strengthen and streamline delivery systems.

(e) Increase in central issue prices of foodgrains should not necessarily be related to rise in minimum support prices. End retail prices should be kept lower than the market prices.

(f) States/UTs should have option to receive their allocation on quarterly basis instead of the present monthly allocations.

The Programme Evaluation Organisation (PEO) of the Planning Commission has suggested that suitable interventions have to be made for effective implementation of RPDS so that the benefits to the desired extent can reach the targeted sections of the society. The major findings of the PEO's evaluation are:

(i) The places suitable for coverage under the scheme, but the ones which has as yet not come into the fold, are to be included under this scheme. In addition, the issue of ration cards should be dealt seriously by eliminating bogus ration cards, issuing ration cards to suitable households and properly replacing the old and dilapidated or lost cards.

(ii) The Food Corporation of India (FCI) should increase and improve its own storing facilities. It should also consider for smaller godown facilities conveniently located near the FPSs run under the RPDS connected with the main FCI godowns so that the commodities may be stored, lifted and distributed easily and timely at regular intervals.

(iii) Along with storing facilities, the door step delivery and the mobile fair price shops should be improved. To reduce the burden of extra cost on commodities (due to addition of high transport cost) and to bring them within the reach of the people for whom it is meant, subsidy should be extended to transport service of RPDS also.

(iv) Considering the local needs and variety of food references of different people, efforts should be made by FCI and local agencies for local procurement of grains acceptable to and preferred by the local people for short term storage and distribution.

(v) All round efforts have to be made to monitor and supervise the working of fair price shops in terms of their (a) Opening time, (b) working hours, (c) regularity in distribution, (d) communication with the consumers. Regular checking is also required to monitor the quality, quantity as well as the prices

of the commodities so that the discrepancies as reported in some cases may be controlled.

(vi) To keep malpractices and temptations down, the margins for the FPS dealers should be fair and reasonable.

Some of the important suggestions have also been made to contribute to the improvement of the viability of the FPS dealer and to assure regular availability to the consumer.

(i) The working hours of the FPS should take into account the convenience of the card holders; e.g. working hours coinciding with office or factory working hours would be in convenient to many people.

(ii) In order to reduce malpractices, increase effectiveness and in keeping with the general objectives, private FPS dealerships should not be given to those whose family business is trading. Instead, unemployed persons should be given the PDS authorisation. Finance on credit should be made available to them for running the FPS.

(iii) The FPS dealers should not be allowed to sell on their private account, the same commodities as are covered by the PDS. Though they should be helped and encouraged, particularly in remote and rural areas, to sell other non-PDS goods from the FPS for improving their turnover, as well to improve the use of their time and overheads.

(iv) Under a system of door-step delivery of supplies to the FPS by the Food and Supplies Department, payment may be collected from the FPS dealers after a week of making deliveries. This step would also reduce the need to visit the Department frequently thereby avoiding the disruption in normal retailing.

(v) Each FPS must display outside the shop its number, working days and hours. similarly, it must also

display the prices of the PDS goods, their stock position, samples of the goods for sale and names and addresses of the members of the local vigilance committee.

(vi) A complaint and suggestion book should also be kept on the counter for each consumer to be able to register complaints without having to ask for it.

(vii) The enforcement staff must periodically check up the records of the FPS and those who violate rules and regulations, must be penalised and debarred from continuing as the FPS dealers.

(viii) Either the FPS should given a subsidy or the profit margins to them, should be increased.

Suggestions given by the Officials of the Agencies engaged in the PDS in Jammu Region

During the survey, the responses have also been generated with regard to other suggestions given by the agencies as exhibited in Tables 6.6, 6.7 and 6.8.

(a) The measures to meet Consumer Preference in terms of taste, variety, colour, etc.

Measures in order of ranking are:

(i) Arrangement of conferences;

(ii) Revamping the vigilance committees;

(iii) Recommendations for more funds; and

(iv) Supervision by the officials.

(b) Improvements in the Organisational and Managerial structure at the District level:

Improvements in order of ranking are:-

(i) Adequate and efficient staff;

(ii) Increase in Commissions;

(iii) Exclusion of high salaried persons;

(iv) Sufficient arrangement; and

(v) Women's participation.

(c)Suggestions to improve the present working of PDS:

Suggestions in order of ranking are:

(i) No. of FPS should be increased;

(ii) Ration quota should be increased;

(iii) Location of FPS should be ideal; and

(iv) Others.

Suggestions Given by FPS dealers

The Fair Price Shop dealers contacted during the survey, have also given responses with regard to the suggestions for effective management of the PDS in Jammu Region. Table 6.9 exhibits that both the urban and the rural respondents have suggested the measures to make this system more effective.

Other suggestions for improvement in the present PDS:

(i) The tasks of issuing and periodical renewal of ration cards should be undertaken on the basis of sending a team of enumerators (including non-official, local representatives). The ration cards should be issued free of cost, or for a nominal charge from at least some groups, at the door-steps of each household.

(ii) Apart from the PDS commodity basket, the FPS should also supply goods produced, procured and marketed by public and cooperative agencies like the NTC, Tea Trading Corporation, Khadi and Village Industries Commission, Cooperative Marketing Federations, etc.

(iii) Good quality properly packed wheat flour should be supplied, particularly in the areas where wheat is relatively less popular.

Table 6.6
Response of the Agencies Regarding Meeting consumer Preference in Terms of Taste, Variety, Co

Response	*Urban* No.	*Urban* %	*Rural* No.	*Rural* %
Yes	15	50.00	12	60.00
No	13	43.33	7	35.00
N.R	2	6.67	1	5
Total	30	100.00	20	100.00

If Yes, the Measures

Ranks	*(i)* *Urban* No. %age	*(i)* *Rural* No. %age	*(ii)* *Urban* No. %age	*(ii)* *Rural* No. %age	*(iii)* *Urban* No. %age	*(iii)* *Rural* No. %age	*(iv)* *Urbal* No. %age	*(iv)* *Rural* No. %age	*(v)* *Urban* No. %age	*(v)* *Rural* No. %age	*Total* *Urban* No. %age	*Total* *Rural* No. %age
I	8	6	5	4	2	0	0	2	0	0	15	12
	53.33	50.00	33.33	33.33	13.33	0.00	0.00	16.67	0.00	0.00	20.00	20.00
II	5	3	9	6	1	3	0	0	0	0	15	12
	33.33	25.00	60.00	50.00	6.67	25.00	0.00	0.00	0.00	0.00	20.00	20.00
III	2	3	1	2	3	3	9	4	0	0	15	12
	13.33	25.00	6.67	16.67	20.00	25.00	60.00	33.33	0.00	0.00	20.00	20.00

(i)	(ii)		(iii)		(iv)		(v)		Total			
Ranks	Urban No. %age	Rural No. %age	Urban No. %age	Rural No. %age	Urban No. %age	Rural No. %age	Urbal No. %age	Rural No. %age	Urban No. %age	Rural No. %age	Urban No. %age	Rural No. %age
IV	0	0	0	0	0	3	1	0	0	0	1	3
	0.00	0.00	0.00	0.00	0.00	25.00	6.67	0.00	0.00	0.00	1.33	5.00
V	0	0	0	0	0	0	0	0	0	0	0	0
	0.00	0.00	0.00	0.00	0.00	0.00	0.00	0.00	0.00	0.00	0.00	0.00
N.R	0	0	0	0	9	3	5	6	15	12	29	21
	0.00	0.00	0.00	0.00	60.00	25.00	33.33	50.00	100.00	100.00	38.67	35.00
Total	15	12	15	12	15	12	15	12	15	12	75	60

Measures

(i) Arrangement of Conferences
(ii) Revamping of Vigilence Committees
(iii) Recommendations for more funds
(iv) Supervision by officials
(v) Checking the weights & measures

Source: As per the survey conducted

Table 6.7

Responses of the Agencies Regarding the organisational structure at the District Level

Responses	*Urban* No.	%	*Rural* No.	%
Year	10.	33.33	9	45.00
Strong	15	50.00	7	35.00
No Response	5	16.67	4	20.00
Total	30	100.00	20	100.00

IF WEAK, THE IMPROVEMENTS

	(i)		*(ii)*		*(iii)*		*(iv)*		*(v)*		*(vi)*		*(vii)*		*(viii)*		*Total*	
----	*Urban* No.	*Rural* No.	*Urban* Nc.	*Rural* No.	*Urban* No.	*Rural* No.	*Urban* No.	*Rural* No.	*Urban* No.	*Rural* No.	*Urban* No.	*Rural* No.	*Urban* No.	*Rural* No.	*Urban* No.	*Rural* No.	*Urban* No.	*Rural* No.
Ranks	*%age*	*%age*	*%age*	*%age*	*%age*	*%age*	*%age*	*%age*	*%age*	*%age*	*%age*	*%age*	*%age*	*%age*	*%age*	*%age*	*%age*	*%age*
I	3	2	2	1	2	1	1	0	0	1	0	1	10	9	14	9	250	200
	30.00	22.22	20.00	11.11	20.00	11.11	10.00	0.00	0.00	11.11	0.00	11.11	100.00	100.00	140.00	100.00	312.50	277.78
II	2	1	3	1	1	1	1	1	1	1	0	0	10	9	28	5	250	200
	20.00	11.11	30.00	11.11	10.00	11.11	10.00	11.11	10.00	11.11	0.00	0.00	100.00	100.00	280.00	55.56	312.50	277.78
III	1	1	2	2	1	1	3	1	1	0	0	1	10	9	23	5	244	196
	10.00	11.11	20.00	22.22	10.00	10.00	11.11	30.00	11.11	10.00	0.00	0.00	11.11	100.00	100.00	230.00	55.56	305.00

	(i)		(ii)		(iii)		(iv)		(v)		(vi)		(vii)		(viii)		Total	
---- Ranks	Urban No. %age	Rural No. %age	Urban No. %age	Rural No. %age	Urban No. %age	Rural No. %age	Urban No. %age	Rural No. %age	Urban No. %age	Rural No. %age	Urban No. %age	Rural No. %age	Urban No. %age	Rural No. %age	Urban No. %age	Rural No. %age	Urban No. %age	Rural No. %age
IV	1	1	1	2	3	3	1	2	1	0	0	0	0	9	24	13	241	192
	10.00	11.11	10.00	22.22	30.00	33.33	10.00	22.22	10.00	0.00	0.00	0.00	100.00	100.00	240.00	144.44	301.25	266.67
V	1	1	0	1	1	1	2	2	1	1	1	1	10	9	21	19	233	191
	10.00	11.11	0.00	11.11	10.00	11.11	20.00	22.22	10.00	11.11	10.00	11.11	100.00	100.00	210.00	211.11	291.25	265.28
VI	1	1	1	1	1	1	2	3	2	2	1	0	10	9	27	13	225	176
	10.00	11.11	10.00	11.11	10.00	11.11	20.00	33.33	20.00	22.22	10.00	0.00	100.00	100.00	270.00	144.44	281.25	244.44
VII	1	1	1	1	1	0	0	0	2	2	2	3	10	9	19	19	216	168
	10.00	11.11	10.00	11.11	10.00	0.00	0.00	0.00	20.00	22.22	20.00	33.33	100.00	100.00	190.00	211.11	272.50	233.33
VIII	0	1	0	0	0	0	0	0	1	1	3	2	5	5	36	31	207	163
	0.00	11.11	0.00	0.00	0.00	0.00	0.00	0.00	10.00	11.11	30.00	22.22	50.00	55.56	360.00	344.44	258.75	226.39
N.R	0	0	0	0	0	1	0	0	1	1	3	1	5	4	23	44	214	203
	0.00	0.00	0.00	0.00	0.00	11.11	0.00	0.00	10.00	11.11	30.00	11.11	50.00	44.44	230.00	488.89	267.50	281.94
Total	10	9	10	9	10	9	10	9	10	9	10	9	80	72	215	158	2082	1689

IMPROVEMENTS

(i) Adequate and efficient staff *(ii)* Sufficient Arrangements *(iii)* Increase in Commission *(iv)* More Funds for more area *(v)* Exclusion of High Salaried Persons *(vi)* FPS licence to unemployed *(vii)* Women in the PDS operation *(viii)* Actions and Legal measures

Source: As per the survey conducted

Table 6.8
Response of the Agencies Regarding Suggestions to Improve the Present Working of PDs

Suggestions	(i)		(ii)		(iii)		(iv)		(v)		(vi)		(vii)		(viii)		Total	
----	Urban No.	Rural No.	Urban No.	Rural No.	Urban No.	Rural No.	Urban No.	Rural No.	Urban No.	Rural No.	Urban No.	Rural No.	Urban No.	Rural No.	Urban No.	Rural No.	Urban No.	Rural No.
Ranks	%age	%age	%age	%age	%age	%age	%age	%age	%age	%age	%age	%age	%age	%age	%age	%age	%age	%age
I	10	6	8	9	3	5	2	0	4	0	2	0	1	0	0	0	30	20
	33.33	30.00	26.67	45.00	10.00	25.00	6.67	0.00	13.33	0.00	6.67	0.00	3.33	0.00	0.00	0.00	12.50	12.50
II	7	9	1	3	3	6	3	2	5	0	1	0	0	0	0	0	30	20
	23.33	45.00	3.33	15.00	10.00	30.00	10.00	10.00	16.67	0.00	3.33	0.00	0.00	0.00	0.00	0.00	12.50	12.50
III	7	9	1	3	3	6	3	2	5	0	1	0	0	0	0	0	30	20
	23.33	45.00	3.33	15.00	10.00	30.00	10.00	10.00	16.67	0.00	3.33	0.00	0.00	0.00	0.00	0.00	12.50	12.50
III	5	3	10	5	4	8	4	0	7	2	0	2	0	0	0	0	30	20
	16.67	15.00	33.33	25.00	13.33	40.00	13.33	0.00	23.33	10.00	0.00	10.00	0.00	0.00	0.00	0.00	12.50	12.50
IV	6	2	0	1	13	1	8	10	3	5	0	1	0	0	0	0	30	20
	6.67	0.00	3.33	5.00	13.33	0.00	33.33	40.00	16.67	45.00	16.67	10.00	6.67	0.00	0.00	0.00	12.50	12.50
V	2	0	1	1	4	0	10	8	5	9	5	2	2	0	0	0	30	20
	6.67	0.00	3.33	5.00	13.33	0.00	33.33	40.00	16.67	45.00	16.67	10.00	6.67	0.00	0.00	0.00	12.50	12.50

	(i)		(ii)		(iii)		(iv)		(v)		(vi)		(vii)		(viii)		Total	
---- Ranks	Urban No. %age	Rural No. %age	Urban No. %age	Rural No. %age	Urban No. %age	Rural No. %age	Urban No. %age	Rural No. %age	Urban No. %age	Rural No. %age	Urban No. %age	Rural No. %age	Urban No. %age	Rural No. %age	Urban No. %age	Rural No. %age	Urban No. %age	Rural No. %age
VI	0	0	0	0	2	0	1	0	0	0	9	7	7	10	0	0	19	17
	0.00	0.00	0.00	0.00	6.67	0.00	3.33	0.00	0.00	0.00	30.00	35.00	23.33	50.00	0.00	0.00	7.92	10.63
VII	9	0	0	1	1	0	1	0	0	0	8	6	2	3	0	0	12	10
	0.00	0.00	0.00	5.00	3.33	0.00	3.33	0.00	0.00	0.00	26.67	30.00	6.67	15.00	0.00	0.00	5.00	6.25
VIII	0	0	0	0	0	0	1	0	0	0	0	1	5	2	12	8	17	11
N.R	0	0	0	0	0	0	0	0	6	4	5	1	13	5	18	12	42	22
	0.00	0.00	0.00	0.00	0.00	0.00	0.00	0.00	20.00	20.00	16.67	5.00	43.33	25.00	60.00	60.00	17.50	13.75
Total	30	20	20	20	30	20	30	20	30	20	30	20	30	20	30	20	240	150

(i) No. of FPS should be increased
(ii) Ration quota should be increased
(iii) Location of FPS should be ideal
(iv) Allotment of Quota should be specific
(v) Ration should be issued on specific No. of Cards
(vi) Increase in Commission
(vii) Providing protection Against Lumpen Elements
(viii) And other

Source: As per the survey conducted.

Table 6.9
Responses Regarding for management of PDS

Suggestions

----	(i)		(ii)		(iii)		(iv)		(v)		(vi)		(vii)		(viii)		Total	
Ranks	Urban No. %age	Rural No. %age	Urban No. %age	Rural No. %age	Urban No. %age	Rural No. %age	Urban No. %age	Rural No. %age	Urban No. %age	Rural No. %age	Urban No. %age	Rural No. %age	Urban No. %age	Rural No. %age	Urban No. %age	Rural No. %age	Urban No. %age	Rural No. %age
I	32	20	26	20	20	26	20	10	2	4	4	0	4	0	4	0	112	80
	28.57	25.00	23.21	25.00	17.86	32.50	17.86	12.50	1.79	5.00	3.57	0.00	3.57	0.00	3.57	0.00	12.50	12.50
II	20	24	18	8	22	10	26	24	12	6	10	6	2	2	2	0	112	80
	17.86	30.00	16.07	10.00	19.64	12.50	23.21	30.00	10.71	7.50	8.93	7.50	1.79	2.50	1.79	0.00	12.50	12.50
III	28	12	18	22	20	20	14	12	16	6	6	8	6	0	4	0	112	80
	25.00	15.00	16.07	27.50	17.86	25.00	12.50	15.00	14.29	7.50	5.36	10.00	5.36	0.00	3.37	0.00	12.50	12.50
IV	12	6	20	16	14	10	24	24	16	6	16	4	2	6	2	2	106	74
	10.71	7.50	17.86	20.00	12.50	21.43	30.00	14.29	7.50	14.29	5.00	1.79	7.50	1.79	2.50	11.83	11.56	
V	2	2	8	0	14	8	14	6	32	34	18	4	8	4	4	4	100	62
	1.79	2.50	7.14	0.00	12.50	10.00	12.50	7.50	28.57	42.50	16.07	5.00	7.14	5.00	7.14	5.00	3.57	5.00
VI	4	2	16	10	16	2	0	0	12	4	22	28	8	0	2	0	80	46
	3.57	2.50	14.29	12.50	14.29	2.50	0.00	0.00	10.71	5.00	19.64	35.00	7.14	0.00	1.79	0.00	8.93	7.19

---- Ranks	Urban No. %age	Rural No. %age	Urban No. %age	Rural No. %age	Urban No. %age	Rural No. %age	Urban No. %age	Rural No. %age	Urban No. %age	Rural No. %age	Urban No. %age	Rural No. %age	Urban No. %age	Rural No. %age	Urban No. %age	Rural No. %age	Urban No. %age	Rural No. %age
VII	6	6	2	2	2	0	10	0	2	0	4	0	40	16	2	2	68	26
	5.36	7.50	1.79	2.50	1.79	0.00	893	0.00	1.79	0.00	3.57	0.00	35.71	20.00	1.79	2.50	7.59	4.06
VIII	2	0	2	0	2	0	2	0	4	0	4	0	2	2	34	10	52	12
	1.79	0.00	1.79	0.00	1.79	0.00	1.79	0.00	3.57	0.00	3.57	0.00	1.79	2.50	30.36	12.50	5.80	1.88
N.R	6	8	2	2	2	4	2	4	16	20	28	30	40	50	58	62	154	180
	5.36	10.00	1.79	2.50	1.79	5.00	1.79	5.00	14.29	25.00	25.00	37.50	35.71	62.50	51.79	77.50	17.19	28.13
Total	112	80	112	80	112	80	112	80	112	80	112	80	112	80	112	80	896	640

Suggestions

(i) Improvements in quality of all the items
(ii) Supervision by food inspectors
(iii) Promotion of 'PDS programme' on a large Scale
(iv) Opening of more FPSs
(v) Improvement in Public Relations
(vi) Timely Availability of ration items
(vii) Provision of law against dishonest dealers
(viii) Enhancements in commission of dealers

Source: As per the survey conducted

Note:

	Urban	Rural
Total No. of Respondents	118	82
No response	6	2
	112	80
No. of Responses generated		

(iv) The ration scales should not be changed frequently and whenever such changes become inevitable, there should be widesprcad dissemination of the information through the media.

(v) The quality of the PDS supplies should be improved and it is necessary to initiate measures for proper grading, cleaning and standardisation.

(vi) To avoid delay in disbursement, goods should be pre-weighed and pre-packed and kept ready for delivery.

(vii) Consumer Councils should be established and their functioning should be effective so as to increase the socio-economic awareness of the public and to induce their participation in the programme of PDS.

(viii) All the household goods required by the rural households should be distributed under the PDS.

(ix) Ration dealership should not be given to the Village VIPs or their relatives. It should be given to the educated persons belonging to the Scheduled Castes and Scheduled Tribes.

(x) Supply should be regular and made under Govt arrangement by using departmental vehicles or by hiring mules, etc. for inaccessible areas.

(xi) All FPSs should be issued commodities at a well-known fixed date so that the card holders can know when the supply is available at FPS.

(xii) A Computer Based Model for monitoring the PDS in all the States and Union Territories has been prepared by the Central Government in consultation with the National Informatics Centre. The model entails computerisation of the operations of Food and Civil Supplies Department in all States and Union Territories for speedy transmission of data. It is also needed to improve the data collection

processes from the districts and blocks to put in place a 'very effective' monitoring system without which, it would be impossible to implement the programmes like the RPDS in a better way.

(xiii) The present PDS should be linked with the employment programmes as these would be useful for strengthening the infrastructure in the states.

(xiv) An efficient PDS would need to determine both the size and the composition of its stocks on the basis of the requirements of the poorer sections of the society.

(xv) Incentives to farmers should be provided through instruments other than price. It will also be necessary to develop an effective insurance scheme to help farmers cope with prices that could fluctuate quite rapidly. Any attempt to create an effective public distribution system would thus has to be linked to a comprehensive package of measures for agriculture, if it is to be both humane and politically viable.

(xvi) Last, but not the least, we should have a look at the Management Information System (MIS). MIS, as it exists now, suffers from many deficiencies. There is really no information flow between top and bottom, resulting in mismatch of requirement, supplies and delivery. Ration cards are attached and detached from one FPS to another without the supply wing of the Governmentbeing aware of it. There is disruption in supplies or changes in allocations without inspectors, FPS owners or PDS beneficiaries Knowing about it or the reasons. It is, therefore, necessary to develop an appropriate MIS. It should clearly earmark areas which require routine/regular information flow and those which require exception reporting. It is necessary to be selected in identifying critical areas and in laying

down the information needs in such selected areas. Procedures and documentation will also need to be standardised. The role of each of the various involved agencies should also be demarcated clearly and interaction between various agencies formalized for easy monitoring and effective co-ordination.

Considering all these aspects, it is possible now to propose a reorganisation of the public distribution system as a national scheme with the participation of the Central, State and Local Governments.

The Various Aspects of the PDS should be as under:

(i) The Central Governments may continue with the present PDS with the procurement and distribution of foodgrains through the FCI at Central Issue Prices (CIP). In addition to this current system, the Central Government should offer a further scheme to distribute additional foodgrains to be supplied to 30 per cent of the people below the poverty line at roughly four kilograms per capita per month and at price which is equivalent to half the market price.

(ii) The State Governments should take the responsibility of delivering this food from the FCI godowns to the fair price shops and which would operate under the supervision and direct charge of the local panchayats.

(iii) The identification of the poor and the targeting of the distribution under this special scheme would be the responsibility of the State Governments.

(iv) The State Governments can ask the local panchayats to identify the poor according to some criteria. If the number of the poor shown up by the panchayats and accepted by the state Government, turn out to be higher than the estimates of the Central Government, the State Govt should bear the burden

of providing the additional food at half the market price after buying the cereals from the FCI at CIP.

(v) The Banking system can also be galvanised to help financing the local level operations. With the gain in experience, the method of targeting can be made perfect and the share of the non-poor can be reduced substantially over time and the improvement in this system can be accelerated.

Thus, the recommendations made in the concluding part of this study may involve hard decisions yet these decisions cannot be postponed further. In the coming decades, with the economy being freed of restrictions, it will be necessary to maintain subsidies on foodgrains at levels that are sustainable by the Government and the economy and yet help poor households in a real way. In order to ameliorate the deprivations of the poor during the process of liberalisation, PDS has to be an effective safety-net. If the consumption levels of foodgrains by the poor are not protected and improved, the reform process itself would have no meaning for people of the country, for the State and the Jammu Province.

Bibliography

Books

1. Aggarwal, R.D. — *Organisation and Management*, Tata McGraw Hill Publication Co, New Delhi, 1984.
2. Bajpai, S.R. — *Methods of Social Survey and Research*, Kitab Ghar, Rampur, 1960.
3. Bapna, S.L. — *Food Security Through The PDS*—The Indian Experience, (in D.S.Tyagi and V.S.Vyas Ed.), *Increasing Access to Food—The Asian Experience*, Sage Publications, New Delhi, 1990.
4. Bardhan, P.K. — *The Pattern of Income Distribution in India—A Review in Poverty and Income Distribution in India*, Statistical Publishing Society, Calcutta, 1974.
5. Best, John. — *Research in Education*, Prentice Hall of India Pvt. Ltd., Fourth Edition, New Delhi, 1982.
6. Bhabswan, E.J. — *Poverty—Encyclopedia of Social Sciences*, The McMillan Company and The Free Press, 1968.

7. Bhatia, B. M. — *India's Food Problem and Policy since Independence*, Somaiya Publications, Bombay, 1970.

8. Bhushan, Y.K. — *Fundamentals of Business Organisation and Management*, 9th Revised & Enlarged Edition, Sultan Chand & Sons, New Delhi, 1981.

9. Blacock, H.M. — *Introduction of Social Research*, Egle Wood Cliffs, Prentice Hall of India Pvt. Ltd., 1970.

10. Chakarvarty, S. — *Development Planning—The Indian Experience*, Oxford University Press, New York, 1988.

11. Datt, Ruddar & K.P.M. Sundharam. — *Indian Economy*, S. Chand & Co., New Delhi, 1981.

12. Dantwala, M.L. — *India's Food Problem*, Asia Publishing House, Bombay, 1960.

13. Dholakia, N & R. Khurana — *Public Distribution System*, Oxford and IBH Publishing CO., New Delhi, 1979.

14. Gupta, Arvind — *Public Distribution of Food Grains in India*, Monograph No. 69, Centre for Management in Agriculture, Indian Institute of Management, Ahmedabad, 1977.

15. Gupta, S.C. — *Food Prices in India*, Meenakshi Prakashan, Meerut, 1970.

16. Kabra, K.N. & A.C. Ittyerah. — *The PDS in India*, Eastern Books, New Delhi, 1992.

17. Koontz, Harold et.al. *Essentials of Management*, Fourth Edition, McGraw Hill International Editions.

18. Kothari, R.C. *Research Methodology-Methods and Techniques*, Wiley Eastern Ltd., New Delhi, 1989.

19. Massie, Joseph.L. *Essentials of Management*, Prentice Hall of India Pvt. Ltd, New Delhi, 1987.

20. Mathur, B.C. et.al *Management in Government*, Publications Division, Ministry of Information and Broadcasting, Govt. of India, 1981.

21. Mongia, J.N. *India's Economic Development Strategies 1951 to 2000 A.D.*, Allied Publishers, New Delhi, 1986.

22. Nawani, N. P. *Towards Food For All-Ideas For a New PDS*, Ministry of Information and Broadcasting, Govt of India, New Delhi, 1995.

23. Ojha, Ghanshyam Das *Organisation and Management of PDS*, Mittal Publications, New Delhi, 1987.

24. Oppen-hein, A.N. *Questionnaire Design and Attitude Measurement*, Hein Maun, London, 1966.

25. Rao, K.V. *Research Methodology in Commerce and Management*, Sterling Publishers Pvt Ltd., New Delhi, 1993.

26. Sadhu, A.N. & A.Singh *Research Methodology in Social Sciences*, Himalaya Publishing House, Bombay, 1980.

27. Sethna, B.N. & L.Groeneveld — *Research Methods in* Marketing *Marketing and Management*, Tata McGraw Hill Publishing Co, Ltd., New Delhi, 1984.

28. Sherlekar, S.A. — *Modern Business Organisation and Management*, Himalaya Publishing House, Bombay, 1987.

29. Sinha, S.L.N. — *Inflation in India*, Vora and co. Publishers Pvt. Ltd., Bombay, 1974.

30. Singh, V.B. — *Evaluation of Fair Price Shops*, Oxford and IBH Publishing Co., New Delhi, 1973.

31. Somasekhara, N — *State's Planning in India*, (Techniques, Procedure and Management)", Himalaya Publishing House, Bombay, 1984.

32. Suryanarayana, G. — *PDS in India*, Chugh Publication, Allahabad, 1985.

33. Taimini, K.K. — *Studies in Retailing Consumer's Co-operation and PDS*, Harshad Prakashan, Pune, 1975.

34. Tyagi, D.S. — *Managing India's Food Economy*, Sage Publications, New Delhi, 1990.

35. Venugopal, K.R. — *Deliverance From Hunger—The PDS in India*, Sage Publications, New Delhi, 1992.

36. Verma, B.N. — *PDS—Theoretical Perspectives*, Uppal Publications, 1990.